THE
POCKET GUIDE
TO
Brilliance

BART KING

Illustrations by Remie Geoffroi

GIBBS SMITH
TO ENRICH AND INSPIRE HUMANKIND
Salt Lake City | Charleston | Santa Fe | Santa Barbara

First Edition
13 12 11 10 09   5 4 3 2 1

For a full bibliography for this book, please go to the author's
Web site: www.bartking.net

Published by
Gibbs Smith
P.O. Box 667
Layton, Utah 84041

Orders: 1.800.835.4993
www.gibbs-smith.com

Designed by Black Eye Design
Printed and bound in Canada
Gibbs Smith books are printed on either recycled, 100% post-
consumer waste or FSC-certified papers.

Library of Congress Cataloging-in-Publication Data

King, Bart, 1962-
   The pocket guide to brilliance / Bart King ; illustrations by
Remie Geoffroi. — 1st ed.
      p. cm.
  ISBN-13: 978-1-4236-0504-1
  ISBN-10: 1-4236-0504-7
  1. United States—History—Miscellanea. 2. United States—
Biography—Anecdotes. 3. Intellect—Anecdotes. 4. United
States—History—Humor. I. Title.
  E179.K495 2009
  973—dc22
                                        2008042102

To the brilliant

people of Mensa.

★★★

(Now will you let me join?)

ACKNOWLEDGMENTS

★★★

I worked very hard on this book—oops, hang on, I dropped my crayon. But I also enlisted a number of learned academics for their assistance. These people now get their fondest reward: their name in a list.

My thanks to Lynn King, Neil van Natta, Kent Meisel, Deena Stach, Seamus Ryan, Lt. Col. Melinda Grow, Mariam Kanso, Col. Gordon Bowen, Jennifer Knuths, Andrew Simon, Rich Patterson, Suzanne Taylor, Courtney Rottgering, and Jared Smith.

If you read anything in this book that makes you unhappy, it is their fault. (But feel free to send any compliments or financial opportunities to me at kingbart@comcast.net.)

CONTENTS

★★★

Introduction

When I told my mother I was working on a book about brilliance, I thought it would make her proud. But as Mom's blows rained down on me, I realized my mistake.

"Will each copy of the book"—*thwack!*— "come with a boredom suppressant"— *pow!*—"so that someone actually reads the blasted thing?"—*kerrang!*—she demanded.

At that moment, I realized two things: first, Mom had a mean right hook, and second, I needed to share my definition of brilliance with her.

Brilliance is one of the greatest of all civic virtues. After all, the more brilliant citizens a nation has, the better off it is! That's why free public education is available in the United States, most of Europe, and in countries as diverse as Sri Lanka and Australia. These are nations aspiring to well-informed, insightful citizens who make intelligent decisions in the voting booth, the workplace, and the condiments aisle of the supermarket.[1]

This book has been specially designed by scientists to cultivate your brilliance and to encourage you to be a more engaged citizen. It does this by shining a light on the United States. Not everyone has considered Americans as being brilliant. Innovative, yes. Inventive, yes. Invasive, occasionally. Brilliant? Not so much.

---

1. *One false move there can be more dangerous than you think. The* relish, *my goodness, the* relish!

Benjamin Franklin was certainly a bright fellow, but he once described a group of typical Americans as "little better than Dunces and Blockheads."

My, that Franklin was a rascal! But I believe he was only partially correct, and so the pages that follow are filled with instructive examples of geniuses, leaders, and dunderheads, who together will guide us toward an understanding of what real "brilliance" is.

I know what you're thinking: "Is this some kind of tricky self-improvement plan? *Bor-ring*." Not at all! Learning what happened *when* and *to whom* not only captures the imagination, it's also FUN. This book will make you look on today's world in a new way, helping you make brilliant conversation—and giving you a safer experience in the condiment aisle!

So keep reading and leave the relish to me.

Quick Wits
and Canny Minds

"I AM THANKFUL FOR LAUGHTER, EXCEPT FOR WHEN MILK COMES OUT OF MY NOSE." —Woody Allen

A grandmother is watching her grandson playing on the beach at Coney Island. Suddenly, a huge wave crashes onto the shore and washes the boy out to sea.

The grandmother lifts her hands to the sky and pleads, "Please God, save my only grandson. Please, I beg of you, bring him back to me!"

Astoundingly, another huge wave rolls in and washes the boy back onto the beach, as good as new. His grandmother looks back up to the heavens and cries, "He had a hat!"

That's one of my favorite jokes by comic Myron Cohen (1902–1986). My guess is that Myron was a pretty bright guy. After all, he wrote his own material, and having a sense of humor is an important part of being brilliant.[1]

Don't believe it? Abraham Lincoln had the best sense of humor of any American president, and his brilliance is unquestioned. (So don't question it!) For example, he once watched as a woman wearing a plumed hat slipped and fell on her backside into a puddle. Before offering his assistance, Lincoln remarked to his companion, "Reminds me of a duck. Feathers on her head, down behind."

---

1. *Never mind that a genius named Isaac Newton supposedly laughed only once in his life.*

How to Tell a Joke

1. Approach slowly, showing your hands so it's clear no harm is intended.

2. Slyly determine the person's political opinions, e.g., "How about that Supreme Court, huh?"

3. Use the information you gather to amuse the person without insulting or pandering to them.

4. Watch for inappropriate signs. These include grimaces, muttering, and the hurling of diesel fuel and/or wheat grass juice.

Still not convinced there's a connection? Well, the *Journal of General Psychology* published a study that found "a positive relationship between intelligence and joke comprehension." See, I have evidence. (Don't get used to it, though.)

As missionaries and traders, French travelers to North America had less interest than other Europeans in stealing Indian lands. Further, the French often chose to learn about and live among Indians, which led to friendships, alliances, and humor.

For example, Indians are relatively hairless, and they found the notion of a beard to be completely *freakish*. That's why one Huron man stared into a Frenchman's bearded face with extraordinary attention for a long time.

The Huron finally broke his silence, exclaiming, "Oh, the bearded man! Oh, how ugly he is!" French settlers seized on this Huron horror of the hirsute, and told the Huron that European *women* had beards too.

You can imagine the Huron's reaction to *that* news.

Even a topic as boring as the weather could be a source of intercultural laughter. In 1728, a Virginian named William Byrd wrote about a conversation he overheard between an Englishman and an Indian. The Indian asked what caused thunder during rainstorms.

The Englishman replied that the god of the English was shooting his gun at the gods of the Indians.

Playing along, the Indian observed that his gods must be frightened by this, as they could then not "hold their water."

As for the Puritans, they were not a barrel of laughs. If a Puritan slipped on a banana peel, rather than making a joke, he and everyone else would wonder what he had done to deserve God's punishment. ("This banana peel doth reek of brimstone!")

But Puritans and other religious immigrants were often businesspeople. So the idea of a religious person who would *never* cheat (unless it was to his or her advantage!) got a lot of mileage in early America.

For example, there's the one about a pious couple who ran a grocery store in Massachusetts. Before settling down in the evening, the wife asked her husband, "Have you added sand to the sugar? Put lard in the butter? Tossed some flour in with the ginger?" she asked.

"Yes, dear," her husband responded.

"Then come in for prayers."

A Hobgoblin Resideth in My Colon

American colonists ate a lot of pork, cabbage, and grain. In short, they had bad gas, as William Byrd (1674–1744) pointed out in his poem "Upon a Fart":

Gentlest blast of ill concoction,
The reverse of the ascending belch;
The only stink avoided by Scotsman,
Beloved and practiced by the Welsh.

Softest note of inward griping,
A reverence's finest part,
So fine it needs no wiping,
Except if it's a brewer's fart.

Swiftest ease of inner pain,
Vapor from a secret stench,
It's rattled out by the unbred swain[1]
But whispered by the bashful wench.

Shapeless fart! We never can show you
But in that merry sport
By which, by burning, we know you
To the amazement of all in court.

---

1. *A country youth.*

YANKEE DOODLE

Civilized folk (like the British) had the impression that colonial Americans were hicks, which brings us to the Yankee Doodles. The music for what became "Yankee Doodle" was composed around 1755 by a British Army surgeon. The tune is the same as the one you know, but the original words were different:

DOLLY BUSHEL LET A FART

JENNY JONES SHE FOUND IT

AMBROSE CARRIED IT TO THE MILL

WHERE DOCTOR WARREN GROUND IT.

About twenty years later, the term "Yankee Doodle" came to mean any numbskull living in New England. Soon, the tune sported new lyrics about a Yankee Doodle, and it became a favorite marching song of the British Army. But after the Battle of Bunker Hill, the rebels began playing it themselves, and by 1776, the "macaroni" lyrics to the tune appeared on the scene. Why macaroni? There are some mysteries in life that will never be explained.

"Frontier humor" also dominated the American landscape, with countless jokes about people moving to where they thought there would be rivers of milk and honey. (This would be pretty disgusting: "Ma, I caught a buttermilk trout!")

As territories became states, the ribbing of particular states became common, as in, "What do divorces and hurricanes in West Virginia have in common? Either way, someone's going to lose a trailer."

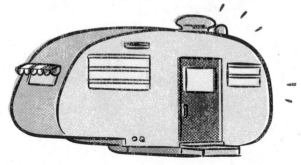

17

PICTURE PERFECT

Zebulon Vance was the Confederate governor of North Carolina. After the Civil War, he was imprisoned for a short time, received a pardon, and was later elected to the Senate. But his Yankee colleagues enjoyed joking with him about his past. While visiting in Massachusetts, Vance reportedly went into an outhouse where a picture of Confederate general Robert E. Lee was hanging. Upon Vance's return, the men asked if he'd seen the bathroom portrait. He told them its location made sense, because "If ever a man lived who could scare the dung out of the Yankees, that man was Robert E. Lee."

Foreigners have noted that American humor has a strong element of pain, cruelty, and death in it. Do you remember the "dead babies" jokes of

Infuriation Nation

Research who a person's least-favorite historical figure is. Does your neighbor start angrily squintin' when you mention Bill Clinton? Is your Uncle Stu upset about Spiro Agnew? Know any piano movers who get steamed by Herbert Hoover?

Get a small framed picture of that not-so-special someone and sneak it onto your target's mantle, desk, or bedside ... Anywhere with enough clutter that the photo won't be spotted immediately. If you're patient, you'll have the last laugh! (And somewhere, Herbert Hoover will be smiling too.)

the 1960s? (Neither do I![2]) And let's not pretend this is relegated to the distant past. My own neighbor told me a joke that qualifies as the worst knock-knock joke in history:

---

2   Example:
      Q: *What's red and swings?*
      A: *A baby on a meat hook.*

KNOCK, KNOCK.

WHO'S THERE?

9/11.

9/11 WHO?

YOU SAID YOU'D NEVER FORGET!

Along the lines of unlikely subjects for humor, after Apache war chief Geronimo surrendered to the United States in 1886, he lived the rest of his life as a prisoner of war. Even so, Geronimo was granted some remarkable freedoms.

General Leonard Woods related how Geronimo once asked to inspect the general's rifle. Looking it over, Geronimo then asked for some bullets. A little anxious, the general courteously showed him how to load and fire the gun.

Geronimo fired at a target and nearly hit a man passing by. As Woods wrote,

Geronimo "regarded [this] as a great joke, rolling on the ground and laughing heartily, 'Good gun!'"

In 1876, writer S. S. Cox analyzed some of the unique traits of American humor. He noted that Americans were known for putting their feet up on furniture, spitting tobacco, and constantly exaggerating. Cox described the traveling American as someone who "leaves his trail on every mountain-pass, his axe-stroke in every forest."

For African Americans, humor has historically been a way to cope with a society that denied them their rights. As Frederick Douglass wrote, when he found himself in unfriendly places, he was greatly helped by his "tendency to see the funny side of things."

The black humor tradition often makes fun of injustices and has an unsurprising dollop of anger and frustration. For example, black writer Paul Beatty once

Good Point!

In the 1800s, a group of religious leaders lobbied in favor of expanding the United States. Their argument was that Manifest Destiny was on their side because the United States is a Christian country.

"So is hell," Mark Twain responded.

observed that one of the funniest things he ever heard was an interview with football star Jim Brown. The ex-athlete was getting angrier and angrier about the questions he was being asked.

When the interviewer suggested Brown take an anger management class, Brown answered, "What are you talking about, man? I *teach* anger management!" (And he did, too.)

The Pocket Guide to Mischief describes the Scottish tradition of flyting, which was an insult contest designed to show off a person's deadly wit. Because slaves were rarely taught to read and write, verbal skills and storytelling were emphasized in early black culture. This helps to explain "the Dozens," the practice of verbally dissing an opponent by saying cruel things about his or her mother and other close relatives. For groups like the Puritans, comparing someone's mom to an unpleasant set of freakish circumstances would have resulted in BIG trouble.

SOME MODERN EXAMPLES OF THE DOZENS INCLUDE:

YO MAMA'S SO BIG, HER OATMEAL BOWL COMES WITH A LIFEGUARD.

YO MAMA'S SO FAT, SHE'S GOT SMALLER FAT WOMEN ORBITING AROUND HER.

YO MAMA'S SO UGLY, WHEN SHE JOINED AN UGLY CONTEST, THEY SAID, "SORRY, NO PROFESSIONALS."

YO MAMA EATS SO MUCH, WHEN SHE GOES TO AN ALL-YOU-CAN-EAT BUFFET, THEY HAVE TO INSTALL SPEED BUMPS.

You get the idea. Writer H. Rap Brown has pointed out that the practice of "signifying" is a more humane practice than the Dozens. In signifying, you can rip on your opponent (instead of his or her mother). For example: "If I had your face, I'd give my head away."

If you're signifying, you can also make yourself sound great: "I might not be the best in the world, but I'm in the top two, and my brother's getting old."

It's not hard to trace a line from boasting to signifying to the rap and hip-hop music movements. You know, like "I'm smooth and wise, the skills I utilize / Lyrics all advanced, you'd think my brain was computerized" (Lord Finesse, 1992). That's much more impressive than rapper T. I.: "T. I., they call me 'Candle Guy' / Probably cuz I am on fire." Or the guys in Clipse, who rap that they're "the black Martha Stewart / Let me show you how to do it." But even Clipse boasts better than Mase: "Young, black and famous / with money hangin' out the anus."

Ahem.

United States citizens who constantly refer to their cash and possessions are following in the steps of an old American tradition. Yes, stupidity, but also being fixated on MONEY. In the 1830s, visiting Frenchman Alexis de Tocqueville observed, "I know of no country, indeed, where the love of money has taken a stronger hold on the affections of men." American writer Washington Irving agreed when he assessed his fellow citizens and decided that the "almighty dollar [was the] great object of universal devotion."

Jews have made an outsized contribution to American humor. In 1982, a *New York Times* reporter estimated that about

Texas: It's Like a Whole Other Country

There are fifty states in the United States, and each of them has a motto. In a pretentious flourish, many of these mottoes are in foreign languages like Greek, Latin, and Hawaiian. With the exception of New Hampshire ("Live free or die"), most mottoes are not particularly inspirational or even accurate.

Folks living in rival states need to be deflated at every opportunity, and here's one now! Learn the motto of a state that borders yours. (If you are outside the United States, go ahead and pick California.) Now alter the motto slightly or entirely. For example, New Hampshire's new motto might be "Live free or pie," "Live free or don't," or "Live free or *my my, this is funny.*"

In addition to official mottoes, all states have at least one slogan. These slogans are intended to promote tourism. Thus, we have Wisconsin's slogan, "Stay Just a

QUICK WITS AND CANNY MINDS

Little Bit Longer." (A little needy, don't you think?) And Missouri has pulled in valuable spelunking dollars by declaring itself "The Cave State."

Riff on existing state slogans or just make up a brand new one. A time-honored example of this would be "Arizona: It's Dehyd-rific!"

Other possibilities:

"New Jersey: Non-Hypoallergenic—Come See for Yourself!"

"Pennsylvania: Baking Crumpets with Clean Coal Technology Since Yesterday!"

"Washington: There's Nothing to Do Here After Ten AM!"

75 percent of stand-up comedians in the United States were Jewish, although the Jewish percentage of the general population was between 2 and 3 percent of the total population!

United States Foreign Policy Explained

Three Boy Scouts reported their good deed of the day to their scoutmaster. "We helped an old lady across the street," said one.

"Okay," said the scoutmaster. "But why do all *three* of you take credit for the good deed?"

"Well," the Scouts explained, "she didn't want to go."

Historically, Jewish humor has often played off being a minority in a non-Jewish ("Gentile") population. Jewish jokes have often included Gentiles suspicious of the education and business skills of Jews. These jokes are unique in that they often make fun of Jews themselves (as opposed to another group). This is funny and also a subtle way of saying, "If we can laugh at ourselves, why should you be prejudiced toward us?"

In 1870, New York's first elevated railway opened in Manhattan. It had been running for about a month when, one day, a big Gentile got on a car and took the only available seat. He looked over and saw that he was next to a Jewish woman.

"Excuse me, but I've always wondered," the man said. "Why are Jews so much cleverer than everyone else?"

The woman thought for a moment as the El rattled along, and finally said, "It might be because of all the herring we eat." At that, the woman took a piece of herring out of a bag and began to eat it.

"How much do you want for the rest of the herring in that bag?" the man asked.

"Ten dollars," she replied. The transaction was made, and the man began eating a herring. Then he stopped mid-bite. "This is crazy," he said. "I could have bought all this herring for much cheaper at the next stop!"

"You see," said the woman. "It's working already!"

MAKING A DIFFERENCE

Your local politicians work hard! To let them know you appreciate it, buy a large number of postcards. Every Monday, write a clean, tasteful joke on the back of one of the cards. Then mail it to your representative, senator, or other local official. Continue this practice for his or her full term of office. The ray of sunshine you'll bring into this politician's life may inspire him or her to initiate some useful legislation. Plus, who knows? Maybe you'll be offered a good job as a speechwriter (or perhaps there's an opening in the mail room!).

Plymouth Rocks

Here's a question for you. Non-English explorers hiked over and sailed around some of the states that became part of the United States before English colonists arrived on the scene. Exactly how many future states did they visit?

A. 9
B. 24
C. 51

The correct answer is B! *¡Este libro debería ser escrito en Español!* Yes, you *should* be reading this book in Spanish. Or perhaps Portuguese, French, or Italian.

Sure, you can start with a lost Italian named Cristoforo Colombo (aka "Christopher Columbus") working for the Spanish and then getting discovered by American Indians. Sure, Indians discovered Columbus! Why does he always get to discover them?

Or maybe you want to skip to another Italian, Giovanni Caboto (better known as "John Cabot"), one of the first Europeans to set foot on the North American continent.

How Brilliant Are You?

Match these answers.

1. FOUNDED THE FIRST SETTLEMENT IN WHAT BECAME
   THE UNITED STATES

2. FIRST PERMANENT SETTLERS OF WHAT BECAME
   THE UNITED STATES

3. REALLY BAD SPORTS

4. THE FIRST PILGRIMS

5. PROBABLY THE MOST OPEN-MINDED SETTLERS

A. JEWS

B. SPANIARDS

C. AFRICAN AMERICANS

D. DUTCH

E. VENUSIANS

Answers:

1. *B. THE SPANISH* built the first overseas settlement in 1526. It was the ill-fated colony of San Miguel de Guadalupe. Founded by Spanish explorer Lucas Vásquez de Ayllón, it was near what is now Cape Fear in North Carolina.

2. *C. AFRICAN AMERICANS* were the first *permanent* settlers of what became the United States. They were slaves at San Miguel de Guadalupe. When the Spaniards bailed out on the settlement, they left their African slaves behind!

3. *B.* How do you say "bad sport" in Spanish? When the French established their own colony near Jacksonville, Florida, *THE SPANISH* destroyed it and slaughtered its inhabitants. Why? They didn't want to see the French succeed where they had failed!

4. *A.* The first North American pilgrims may have been *JEWISH*. In late 1492, Jews in Spain were forced to convert to Catholicism or leave the country. There is considerable evidence that descendants of some of the Jews who left Spain ended up in New Mexico a century later. That's a long trip to make for religious freedom! (And even in New Mexico, Jews had to practice in secret.)

5. *D. DUTCH* settlers came from a country that outlawed religious discrimination. Their "New Amsterdam" colony on the south tip of Manhattan was quite tolerant: anybody was welcome to join! Within a few years, more than sixteen languages were spoken there.

Operation Exploration

Obtain a fringed leather jacket or fringed gingham petticoat and pose as the first explorer of your neighborhood. For authenticity, "chart the territory" by hand-drawing a map as you go. Note the customs of locals by logging entries in a fringed leather-bound notebook.

Good quotes to spout:

"I remember when all of this was primeval forest." (Use this in malls and deserts.)

"Ours may be the first human hands to ever set foot here." (Note: This line only works if you're walking on your hands.)

"You people are absolute savages!" (An impressive announcement to make at softball games.)

If you insist on English voyagers, how about Martin Frobisher? In 1577, he made a dangerous voyage to North America and collected tons and tons of gold. He was rich—rich, I tell you! Or, rather, he would have been, but upon returning to England, he found that his gold was actually iron pyrite—"fool's gold."

Astoundingly, Frobisher went *back* to North America and this time brought hundreds of tons of *real* gold back to England. Now he really *was* rich! Right?

Wrong. Fool's gold again! There is no record of Frobisher's response to this news. (I'm guessing it was unprintable.)

The English later founded a colony at Jamestown, Virginia, in 1607. The colonists settled in the middle of Tsenacomacoh, an American Indian nation of over fifteen thousand people. With its villages separated by elm and chestnut forests, the country may have looked uninhabited to the settlers, but the locals were using nearly all of it for hunting, gathering, fishing, and farming.

The Jamestown colony was a private business funded by an English corporation. The colonists were charged with collecting all of the silver and gold believed to be lying around the New World. But the colonists were such an odd assortment of characters—British gentlemen and their servants rubbing

elbows with English vagabonds—their story ended up like some kind of colonial reality TV show.

This motley crew didn't make life easy on themselves. They built Jamestown in a vermin-infested, brackish swamp without fresh water. And they hadn't exactly packed very well for the trip. (One colonist brought a miniature windmill, just for fun.) More than 80 percent of those who moved to Virginia during the next eighteen years died.

In short order, only 38 of the original 104 colonists were alive. By 1610, the settlers had eaten all their pets as well as all the rats and mice in the area. They began to dig up corpses for nourishment. One man killed his wife and salted her for future provisions. Some reality show!

Despite this malnutrition, American colonists refused to eat clams or mussels, and they would only reluctantly snack on salmon, oysters, duck, or scallops. To the north, lobsters could be easily plucked from tide pools, but they were considered fit only for convicted criminals.

Once Powhatan, the chief of Tsenaco-macoh, understood the colonists had designs on his people's land, the relationship between the English and the Indians went downhill fast. Could it be that the English were just misunderstood? After all, they once invited more than two hundred local Indians over for a toast to celebrate "eternal friendship" between their peoples.

The English were apparently just kidding, though. The Indians began dropping dead from the poison that had been put in their "friendship" drinks!

Since there wasn't any gold to be found, the colonists got down to business planting tobacco.

And more and more colonists kept coming and coming . . .

THE INVASION OF THE PUKE STOCKINGS!

Thirteen years after Jamestown's founding (and five hundred miles to the north), the *Mayflower* arrived. By the time the ship set anchor, its seasick passengers had been nicknamed "puke stockings" by the ship's sailors.

Some of these puking passengers were the Puritans who went on to found the Plymouth Colony. Yes, yes, they were very brave to cross the Atlantic. After all, voyagers sometimes took seven months to complete the journey. And making a new home in a strange place was very daunting.

But what's important about these people is that even before they became puke stockings, they smelled *really* bad.

Of course, almost all Europeans stank. Many of them *never* stripped naked and bathed, so some clothing was ALWAYS on their bodies. (And it was usually the

41

same piece of clothing from the day before!) But because Puritans bathed even less than other Europeans, they were especially ripe.

★ *UP UNTIL 1880, ABOUT FIVE OUT OF SIX AMERICANS WASHED WITH A PAIL AND A SPONGE . . . WHEN THEY WASHED AT ALL.*

The Puritans were a religious group that lived in England and Holland during the 1500s and 1600s. They were strict—VERY

42

strict. You could catch a beating for *smiling* in a Puritan church.

Heck, the Puritans even fashioned a wooden ball on a string that they used to bop people on the head. They would only do this if you started to fall asleep during the *really* interesting seven-hour-long sermons they had in church.

Conveniently for *Mayflower* passengers, a plague from Europe had killed about 90 percent of the Indians in the area before their arrival. This got the passengers started on a fun "welcome to New England" activity: grave robbing!

As the new arrivals dug up graves of dead Indians, they found bows, bowls, and other useful items that had been buried so that the deceased could use them in the after-life. Score! Like the Jamestown colonists, the *Mayflower* passengers hadn't packed practical items like plows, fishing lines, or livestock, and so they found the Indian graves particularly useful.

You know what happened next. Even with good countryside and good grave robbing, half of the Pilgrims' landing party died within a few months. They starved, they froze, and they generally dropped dead. The surviving group would probably have died soon enough, but then—*ta-dah!*—Squanto[1] showed up.

"Who's Squanto?" you ask? (If you didn't ask, just play along.) He was an Indian whose hometown was near the spot where the Pilgrims had just settled. In fact, Squanto had just returned home after a long voyage abroad (during which he learned English) only to find that most everyone he knew was dead from the plague.

Since he was basically alone, and since the Pilgrims *seemed* nice enough, Squanto helped them survive. ("Hey, I was in the neighborhood, and I noticed that you were dropping dead . . .") But if Squanto had

---

1.   *His actual name was Tisquantum, but the Pilgrims couldn't pronounce that.*

known that within two years, *he* would also die from European disease, I'm guessing he'd have kept his distance.

But Squanto showed the Pilgrims how to hunt and farm, and he also introduced them to the other surviving Indians, the Wampanoag ("People of the Dawn").

The Pilgrims sent word back to England encouraging other Puritans to come to the New World.

And the Real Estate Wars were underway.

FLUSHING RULES

When Quakers (known as the Society of Friends) arrived in North America, they got a chilly reception from the Puritans. The Plymouth colony quickly outlawed Quakers, and the Puritans were willing to whip, mutilate, and even hang them.

Contrast that with the Dutch, who settled

in New Amsterdam (later known as New York). To oppose discrimination against Quakers, a group of concerned colonists wrote the Flushing Remonstrances. ("Flushing" was the name of the town; it's still in New York. A remonstrance is a "correction.")

The document read, *"We desire . . . not to judge lest we be judged, neither to condemn lest we be condemned, but rather let every man stand and fall to his own master. . . . we are bound . . . to do good unto all men and evil to no man."*

The best thing about it: *nobody* who signed the document was a Quaker! Yep, the Dutch colonists stuck up for someone else simply because it was the right thing to do. This was the first expression of religious tolerance in what became the United States.

The ideas of the Flushing Remonstraces became official policy in New Amsterdam. Good on the Dutch!

LET'S LEARN MORE!

None of the people who sailed on the *Mayflower* had a middle name. But while the idea of a middle name hadn't yet caught on (only three of the first seventeen American presidents had one), the Puritans made up for it by giving their kids monikers like "Kill Sin," "Be-Courteous," and "Praise-God."

Based on your understanding of Puritan culture, list some names a Pilgrim would give a child born today.

Bad Habits

and Funky Customs

"I DON'T HAVE ANY BAD HABITS. THEY MIGHT BE BAD HABITS FOR OTHER PEOPLE, BUT THEY WORK FOR ME."
—*Eubie Blake, American composer*

The American settlers were a rough bunch, and so are their descendants. The next time your great-great-great-grandpappy talks about how much better-behaved folks were back in the good old days, reply thusly:

YOU: I'LL BE A SUCK-EGG MULE, GRAMPS! FOLKS BACK THEN TORE UP THE PEA PATCH EVEN WORSE'N KIDS TODAY!

Anyway, despite straitlaced folks like the Pilgrims, most Americans have historically been fond of smoking, breaking laws, drinking, gambling, and swearing. Wait, what am I saying? The Pilgrims drank beer too!

AN OUT-OF-HOUSE EXPERIENCE

In fact, the Pilgrims probably even drank beer in the outhouse. When nature called, *everyone* used either a chamber pot (if indoors) or an outhouse. Without interior plumbing in their homes, they had no other choice.

A chamber pot (aka Badger, Slop Jar, Looking Glass, or Thunder Mug) was generally kept under the bed. It was definitely the second choice for those in need. It's possible that children looking under someone's bed and finding a filled

Thunder Mug may have started the belief that "there's a monster under my bed!"

As for outhouses, their virtue was in keeping "night soil" entirely out of the house. North American colonists used a number of terms for them, including:

BACKHOUSE: Because it might be located in back of the regular house.

FEDERAL BUILDING: Important business is transacted there.

HOUSE OF OFFICE: Now there's a distinguished-sounding place to bust an all-American grumpy!

JAKES: Like the other outhouse nicknames of Auntie and Biffie, I have no idea why they called it this.

ONE-HOLER: Once you get inside, you have one choice. Use it wisely.

Dookie Defenestration

Before becoming France's king, Louis-Philippe I (1773–1850) visited the United States. At one overnighter, an American host told the future king that no chamber pots were available. To the future monarch's amazement, the host then pointed at the window.

POST OFFICE: Where it's always time to deliver something first class.

PRIVY: An English term for the private place (from the Latin "privus.")

TWO-HOLER: A high-volume outhouse, with room for more than one user.

WHITE HOUSE: I like this. It lends the whole sordid affair a little class.

If you'd like to impress your neighbors, construct an outhouse on your property. (This will especially amaze them if you live in an apartment.) First, pick a shady spot. *Oy,* nothing could be worse than going into an outhouse as hot as a greenhouse.

Next, dig a hole that's four to six feet deep. Any deeper, and you're asking for real trouble should a kid fall in or the outhouse seat collapse under a heavy visitor.

Outhouse holes were typically lined with boards or stone. That's because they would eventually be emptied, either by professional "night soil" removers or by the outhouse owner. The alternative was to let the hole fill up, dig a new hole, and then move the whole outhouse over to the new locale.

When looking over the blueprints for the outhouse, remember to put in windows to bring in light and ventilation. But for privacy, put them up as high as possible!

Finally, before attaching the outhouse door, make sure to cut a vent in it.

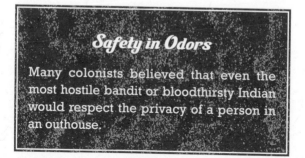

Safety in Odors

Many colonists believed that even the most hostile bandit or bloodthirsty Indian would respect the privacy of a person in an outhouse.

Originally, this could be a crescent moon (signifying a women's outhouse) while a sunburst or star pattern marked a men's room. However, since men never cleaned their outhouses, the ones with suns or stars on the doors soon fell into disrepair, leaving only outhouses with crescent moons for both genders.

As a finishing touch, be sure to put some corncobs in your new outhouse. Hey, you want to be historically accurate, don't you? They didn't have toilet paper back in the day. As poet James W. Riley wrote,

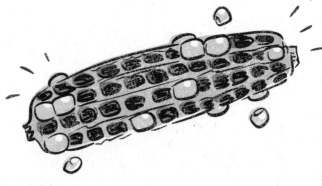

"THE TORTURE OF THAT ICY SEAT COULD MAKE A SPARTAN SOB / FOR NEEDS MUST SCRAPE THE GOOSEFLESH WITH A LACERATING COB."

Toilet paper took a surprisingly long time to catch on. In 1857, an American named Joseph Gayetty came up with the first version of modern toilet paper. Called "Therapeutic Paper," the sheets contained aloe. Good idea. To help spread the word about his product, Gayetty had his name stamped on every sheet. Bad idea. It would be more than thirty years before toilet paper on a roll was available and popular.

Meanwhile, Halloween had gained popularity in the United States as a night to play pranks. Unsurprisingly, outhouses became special targets. Tipping over outhouses (occupied or not) was common. One of young Andrew Jackson's favorite pranks was moving outhouses to parts unknown and then chuckling as those "in need" looked around in horror. Ambitious pranksters would move the entire structure to unlikely spots, like a barn roof!

Many a farmer loaded his shotgun with rock salt and slept lightly on October 31. Tragically, by the start of the twentieth century, most American households either had an indoor bathroom or were going to have one added soon, thus robbing the world of good outhouse stories.

SAGGING, UNDERPANTS, AND OTHER IMPORTANT MATTERS

Try asking someone who's sagging (wearing pants that sag down the hips) where the style came from. According to my survey, the odds are 105 percent that he'll say, "Dunno," "Huh?" or "Mommy, a strange person's asking me about sagging!"

Sagging started off as a fashion statement for prisoners. In the twentieth century, many prisons began issuing baggy clothing with no belts to the inmates. This was done so that the inmates couldn't use their clothing for suicide or weapons. In the 1990s, rappers started to copy the style, wearing loose pajama-type clothes and sagging jeans that revealed their boxers. (The rappers had loose wrappings!)

Since there are a handful of people who copy what rappers do, the style then went out to the general population. Regular people like you and me started sagging. (Yes, I'm sagging as I write this.)

Some saggers have nearly their whole butt hanging out. The day before being elected president, Barack Obama said, "Brothers should pull up their pants." Some cities (and the whole state of Louisiana) have even tried to pass laws against sagging on the grounds that it is "indecent." And schools can enforce dress codes against sagging, just like they can restrict really skimpy clothes and clothing with drug and alcohol references. Another argument follows the same logic used against bad words: sagging represents a destructive, antisocial lifestyle. (Sheesh, what do these people have against criminals?)

But even though sagging looks dopey, maybe it's not the kind of thing that should be made illegal. Seriously—even if you don't like it, you have to admit that sagging is better than its opposite: really *tight* pants!

As for underpants, they've gone through some changes of their own. Early Americans of both sexes often wore wool long johns (aka "union suits") that covered the whole body from neck to feet. (Man, that was some scratchy underwear!) Eventually, cotton two-piecers appeared. Women began wearing bloomers, which started off huge and shrunk to their manageable style today.

Thongs first appeared in 1939, after New York mayor Fiorello LaGuardia insisted that the city's strippers clean up their act. There was no way that strippers were going to wear bloomers, and so butt floss was born.

How a male answers the question "Boxers or briefs?" has to do with how old-school he is about his underpants. Boxers appeared in 1925. Boxers wore them. (You saw that coming, right?) Boxers liked them because the shorts had an elastic waistband, so they didn't have to wear a leather belt in the ring anymore.

(Nothing hurts more than a hook to the belt buckle.)

Ten years later, the first tighty-whities (aka briefs) showed up. Like boxers, they were supposed to be sporty, so they were called "jockeys." They were immediately popular. And to get back where we started, while briefs are currently

Full Moon!

The word "mooning" dates back to college campuses in the 1960s. As you know, it describes a person who taunts another by pulling down his pants and exposing his buttocks. While the *word* is American, the gesture has been around for a long time. The Maoris called this move "whakapohane." It was recorded by a Westerner in 1774, when Captain James Cook wrote that a Pacific Islander "showed us his backside in such a manner that it was not necessary to have an interpreter."

more popular than boxers, nobody sags to show their briefs, although I think that would be pretty funny if they did.

DRINKING

Both tea and coffee were more expensive than almost all types of alcohol until the 1850s. Not only that, but there was no

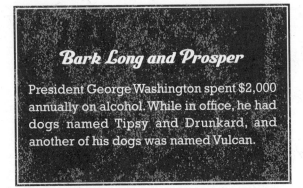

Bark Long and Prosper

President George Washington spent $2,000 annually on alcohol. While in office, he had dogs named Tipsy and Drunkard, and another of his dogs was named Vulcan.

Red Bull available back then. So people drank alcohol. *Lots* of alcohol. In 1830, the average adult drank seven gallons of hard alcohol yearly, which is about seven times more than the current amount.

The colonists and first United States citizens took their drinking seriously. English pioneers thought that drinking booze was healthy and normal. And in a way, they were right about alcohol being good for you. While you can get a nasty little germ drinking bad water, germs tend to die in whiskey bottles. (Actually, *everything* tends to die in whiskey bottles.)

When the United States government tried to put a tax on whiskey, the Whiskey Rebellion broke out in Pennsylvania. (It's a good thing a different drink wasn't taxed; how silly would it look if there had been a Mint Julep Rebellion?) To put down the rebel whiskey drinkers, George Washington sent a force of thirteen thousand soldiers. They were dubbed the Watermelon Army because many of the men came from New Jersey, which is the garden state, and, oh, never mind.

It's Franklin Time

Benjamin Franklin was such an appreciative beer drinker, he wrote, "Beer is living proof that God loves us and wants us to be happy."

Heavy drinkers disgusted their fellow citizens by drooling and singing patriotic songs out of tune. Over time, the opponents of alcohol began to form "temperance" groups, and the political party known as the Know Nothings actively campaigned against booze.

Tea Time? More Rum!

In 1773, a Boston man named Benjamin Edes hosted a meeting of men opposed to an incoming shipment of extremely low-priced British tea. (But why complain about cheap tea at a time when it was so expensive, only wealthy colonists drank it? That's another story.) Benjamin and his son, Peter, set out a huge punch bowl full of rum for the visitors, and Peter had a hard time keeping the bowl full. The men eventually staggered off to dress up as Indians and to start throwing 342 chests of tea from the British ships into Boston Harbor.

This process took several hours, as many of the Boston Tea Partiers were busy blowing chunks into the harbor.

Nationwide, the temperance movement had its ups and downs, and leaders often didn't know what side of the issue to take. For example, there's the politician who was asked for his view on whiskey:

"If by 'whiskey,'" the politician answered, "you mean the devil's brew, the poison scourge, and the bloody monster that destroys innocence, then I am definitely *against* it.

"But if by 'whiskey,'" he continued, "you mean the oil of conversation, the taxes on which brings millions of dollars to build hospitals that provide tender care for little crippled children, then I am *for* it!"

The effort to control drinkers led to the Lager Beer Riot in Chicago. In 1855, Know Nothing mayor Levi Boone put a severe licensing fee on bars. Though the fee was intended to discourage drinking and raise money for the city, a melee broke out upon its passage.

From 1920 to 1933, the making and selling of alcohol was outlawed during Prohibition, which was enacted with the Eighteenth Amendment to the Constitution. During that time, an illegal still that could make 130 gallons of alcohol a day was found on the farm of Senator Morris Shepherd.

This was particularly weird, since he WROTE the Eighteenth Amendment!

The Eighteenth Amendment was later repealed, which meant that Prohibition was prohibited.

MONIKERS

Thankfully, the custom for naming babies has changed over the years. Up until the mid-twentieth century, men had a lot of influence over choosing names for their kids, and the results were not good. In addition to coming up with bad choices like Oswald, Lucretia, and Hazel, men often liked to give their children "funny" names. For example, how many dads have wanted to have a son whose middle name was "Danger"? (That way, the kid could say, "Danger is my middle name." Hmmm, actually, that's pretty cool!)

But here's the problem: studies show that people with odd and ugly names do poorly in school and are both less popular and more likely than "regular" kids to have emotional problems. Hey, don't look at me. Sure, my name is Bart Algae King, but I'm doing fine. Just fine. Sniff.[1]

In fact, I'm doing WAY better than the American kids from the past named Helen Troy, Goblin Fester, Cheese Caesar, and Garage Empty. (*Goblin Fester?* I actually sort of like that!) Historians who have gone through census records have also found that people have named their babies Ogre, Wrath, Lucifer, Medusa, and Ghoul.

---

1. *Hey, if my parents had named me "Art King," I could have been "King, Arthur" on the roll sheets in school!*

CUSSIN' UP A STORM

Picture a country where the people are so intelligent, they never use bad words, expletives, profanity, or Phillips-head screwdrivers. Instead, these brilliant folks are precise with their language, e.g., *"HOW EXTRAORDINARILY UNFORTUNATE THAT I'M DRIVING OFF A CLIFF AT HIGH SPEED."*

Imagine the unimaginable brilliance it would take to never let loose a "Dag nab it!" when you drop your toast and it lands butter-side down. That's apparently the kind of brilliance American Indians had. Most tribes didn't have any swear words until colonists brought them to North America. Not only would colonists provide the expletives, they also gave Indians cause to use them!

But what is it that makes a bad word "bad" in the first place? It turns out that almost all words start off in life as innocent and good. One theory is that some of them start hanging out with the wrong words at the roller-skating rink. Pretty soon, they're playing "crack the whip" and considering more diabolical definitions.

This theory leaves something to be desired. The truth is that humans often start using these same "good" words for different uses. Take "baloney." Baloney only referred to lunch meat until a politician named Alfred Smith said, "No matter how thin you slice it, it's still baloney." Ever since then, an innocent lunch meat came to mean the same thing as "horse puckey."

So *baloney* joined the many other fake swear words that we have in English, like *gosh, jeepers, shucks, blooming, blasted,* and so on. If you think these are too wimpy to have ever been considered as "cussing," think again: in 1941, a lawyer was nearly imprisoned by a federal judge for using a *really* bad word in court. What was the word? "Darn!"

One word that's stronger than "darn" is

the word "crap." This used to be a fine word that anyone could use to signify the stuff found left over in a keg of unfiltered apple juice or at the bottom of a cup of coffee. But crap's definition went to heck. (And no, Sir Thomas Crapper had nothing to do with it.)

Most bad words come in one of these three flavors:

1. *OBSCENITIES:* inappropriate words related to body parts or functions.

2. *PROFANITIES:* words considered offensive to someone's religious beliefs.

3. *SLURS AND OTHER IDIOCIES:* words that insult a person's ethnicity, race, or background.

Speaking of background, why are there so many slurs for people from the country but no similar line of abuse for city dwellers? We've all heard of *hicks, lunkheads, rednecks, bumpkins, hillbillies, brush apes, hayseeds, acorn crackers,*

Presidential Cussing

Many United States presidents have been fond of cussing. There are tapes of Richard Nixon saying things in the Oval Office that would make a sailor blush. But one president kept a pet in the White House that could out-cuss Nixon. Andrew Jackson (president from 1829–1837) taught his pet parrot Pol (short for Polly) all sorts of VERY bad words. When Jackson died, the parrot was kept with Jackson's body to keep him company. Unfortunately, visitors paying their respects to the president were shocked at the parrot's language.

Pol cussed so much at the wake that he eventually had to be removed from the room. *Bad parrot!*

hog rangers, clodhoppers, ridge runners, local yokels, nosebleeds, peckerwoods, turnip suckers, sprout straddlers, and *goober grabbers.* These bumpkins live in places like the *sticks,* the *toolies,* and the *boondocks,* with names like *Hicksville, Jackass Gulch, Southern Succotash, Squash Corner,* and *Cocoahole.*

Cussin' Quiz!

Match the old-school cuss word with the person it would apply to:

1. groper   A. doctor

2. pisspot   B. maverick

3. fart catcher   C. servant

4. s*** sack   D. blind person

Answers: 1.D 2.A 3.C 4.B

Many Americans thought of cussing as a manly activity. It could give a young man "street cred." Being able to "cuss the bark off of a dogwood tree" was thought of as pretty cool, and it even became sort of a compliment to call someone "cussed." It meant that the person was ornery and stubborn.

EXTENDED ACTIVITY

During the Civil War, it became popular among soldiers to use the phrase with the initials "b.s." (Yes, the "b" stands for "bull.") Other popular phrases included *heifer dust, bovine excrement,* and *bushwash.*

For more acceptable ways to express this idea, history provides us with *hogwash, horsefeathers, twaddle, tripe, cock-and-bull, drivel, balderdash, claptrap, rubbish, pap, mumbo jumbo, poppycock, bosh, malarkey, flimflam, flapdoodle, fiddle-faddle, tommyrot, codswallop, gobbledygook,* and *hokum.*

Sadly, many of these words have fallen out of fashion. Try to reintroduce them into circulation by using them as much as possible. Has someone expressed a political opinion that you strongly disagree with? "Poppycock!" Part of the fun is seeing the expression on someone's face when a "Horsefeathers!" pops out of your mouth.

Great Moments in Cussing

Admiral David Farragut (1801–1870) once performed a memorable bit of swearing. His nickname was "Old Salamander" because he wasn't afraid to sail his ships into enemy cannons. (It was believed back then that salamanders could not be harmed by fire.)

During the Civil War, Farragut was commanding a Union fleet of eighteen ships. The fleet was beginning its attack on a Confederate stronghold at Alabama's Mobile Bay, which was booby-trapped with "torpedoes." (That's what they called mines back then.)

When one of Farragut's ships hit a mine, the

explosion caused the other ships to delay their approach. Farragut couldn't see what had happened, and he shouted to the closest ship to find out why the attack was stalled. Farragut was told one of his ships had been torpedoed.

"Damn the torpedoes!" Farragut supposedly cried. "Full speed ahead!"

The rest of the ships continued into the bay, and Farragut's forces won the battle.

Score one for the Old Cussing Salamander.

Talkin' 'Bout a Revolution

"THE HISTORY OF OUR REVOLUTION WILL BE ONE CONTINUED LIE FROM ONE END TO THE OTHER. [IT WILL READ] THAT DR. FRANKLIN'S ELECTRIC ROD SMOTE THE EARTH AND OUT SPRANG GEORGE WASHINGTON. THAT FRANKLIN ELECTRIFIED HIM WITH HIS ROD, AND HENCEFORTH THESE TWO CONDUCTED ALL THE POLICY NEGOTIATIONS, LEGISLATURES, AND WAR." —*John Adams*

Forget electricity; let's talk about powdered wigs. While the American founders wore wigs, they did *not* wear false eyelashes, and for that we can be thankful. But George Washington and most of his male friends did wear make-up. What else can you call it when a man powders and colors his cheeks?

Rich American men wore make-up until 1840, when Martin Van Buren lost his chance at a second presidency after his opponent mocked how many cosmetics he had on his dressing table.

Luckily, fashions change. Think about how much worse it would have been if George W. Bush had been wearing a wig when he spoke to Queen Elizabeth II during her 2007 visit to the White House.

The president said, "You helped our nation celebrate its bicentennial in *17*—" Realizing his mistake, Bush corrected himself and continued, "in *1976*." Queen Elizabeth just glanced up and muttered. Bush later said, "She gave me a look that only a mother could give a child."[1]

Speaking of Independence Day, you may have heard that the American Revolution started with poor colonial farmers banding together to cast off their shackles of taxation without representation. (Those chains sure had a lot of syllables.) *Huzzah!*

But the majority of American colonists *didn't* support the Revolutionary War in any concrete way. Although there were more than two million folks living in the colonies, less than 1 percent of them were willing to join the army. And those who did join were often poor, unmarried teenage boys. To them, the promise of free clothing and meals and $6.50 a month sounded pretty darned good.

Life was actually pretty good for folks

---

1. *That's still better than what Jimmy Carter did. When he was president, he kissed the queen on the lips. She was outraged. (And so was I!)*

throughout the colonies. The colonists had a free press, voted for their local representatives, and were as well educated as the English. The "middle class" (people who make a comfortable living) was about the same size as it is today. In the South, property owners were more concerned with slave rebellions than revolution. With the American population *and* economy regularly doubling in size, the future looked bright.

So which heroic American leader motivated the relatively happy colonists to take up their epic struggle for liberty and the rights of man?

A disgusting Englishman named Thomas Paine.

He really was disgusting. Thomas Paine never *ever* washed. One acquaintance wrote that Paine was "the most abominably dirty being on the face of the earth." Although Paine wasn't referring to his body odor when he wrote, "These are

79

times that try men's souls," his friends might have agreed.

Paine didn't arrive in North America until 1774, but he made up for lost time by penning fiery prose in favor of liberty and rebellion. His 1776 pamphlet *Common Sense* argued that the quarrelsome colonists could and should unite against their common English enemy.

Not everyone loved Paine's project. (John Adams called it a "crapulous mass"!) But *Common Sense* was an uncommonly huge best seller, and as Paine's ideas spread, they eventually got a war started. But Paine somehow used up all the goodwill he should have had by taking a very strong stand against organized religion. His popularity died well before he did in 1809.

Only *six* people attended the funeral of the Father of the Revolution.

Buried in an out-of-the-way plot in New

Hard-Scrabble Times

Folks in the Colonial era sure had it rough. For one thing, they didn't have any good board games. Not only were Candyland and Battleship unheard of, there was no Scrabble! (It was invented by a man named Alfred Butts centuries later.) But you can make up for lost time by playing Colonial Scrabble. This game is played like regular Scrabble, but before you pick up your tiles, someone has to say, "Let's go back to a time when games were more ... civilized." Then commence play. Players score double when they can spell any authentic Colonial word or phrase. (I'll wager a pipkin of whortleberries that you'll have a fine time of it.)

York, Paine was dug up (without permission!) by an Englishman named William Cobbett. Outraged that Paine had been forgotten in the United States, Cobbett took Paine's remains back to England, where a proper monument could be erected.

The idea was to raise funds by taking Paine's body on a tour of England. But Paine was unsurprisingly unpopular in his homeland. He had started the American Revolution! No one paid to see his body, and Cobbett ended up storing Thomas's Paine's body beneath his own bed, until his own death in 1837.[2]

Today, no one knows where the remains of the author of the American Revolution are located.

Back to the Revolution! Most colonists didn't want to join the army, and they didn't want to help feed it, either.

---

2.   *Lord Byron wrote a poem for the occasion: "In digging up your bones, Tom Paine / Will Cobbett has done well / You visit him on earth again / He'll visit you in hell."*

Biting the Bullet

Imagine a time when there were no pain-killers. (Hard to do, since you wouldn't be able to read this book without them!) Soldiers who were wounded in battle usually had their injured limbs amputated. To get them through this agony, a surgeon would strap the soldier down and give him a soft lead bullet to bite into. This reduced screaming and gave the soldier a way to vent. It also gave us the phrase "biting the bullet," which means to take pain like an adult. (So put down those Advil and keep reading.)

Provisions for soldiers in the Continental Army sometimes ran so low that stew was made from melted candles and boiled boots. As you can imagine, this kind of diet had an effect on the army. During a retreat across New Jersey in 1776, the painter Charles Peak ran into an incredibly malnourished soldier. It wasn't until

83

The First Civil War

The Battle of Kings Mountain in South Carolina was one of the strangest things that occurred during the Revolutionary War. Thomas Jefferson called it the "turn of the tide of success." Fought in 1780, the battle pitted *American* revolutionary soldiers against *American* Loyalists who supported the king.

Yep, Americans fighting Americans. No British soldiers were involved! The battle was short and bloody, and then the Loyalists surrendered. About seven hundred of them were captured and then taken on a forced march to captivity. Along the way, so many of these colonists were murdered by their American guards, the revolutionary commander had to issue an order "to restrain the disorderly manner of slaughtering . . . the prisoners."

Nor was this a one-way street. After Benedict Arnold's treachery was discovered, he led Loyalists into battle for the British. When Continental soldiers tried to surrender to the Loyalists, Arnold's men massacred them.

Peak spoke to the soldier that he recognized his own brother.

General Ebenezer Huntington was so disgusted by what cheapskates his fellow colonists were, he said, "I wish I could say I was not born in America."

Another major problem was that the politicians in charge of supplying the Revolutionary Army thought that no one should *profit* from the war. Imagine that! Times really have changed.

By late 1777, George Washington could only watch in despair as thousands of his men walked barefoot and starving in the snow en route to Valley Forge, Pennsylvania. Meanwhile, American farmers sold their crops to the British Army in Philadelphia at excellent prices!

American Adventure: Thaddeus Kosciuszko's Park!

Being a park ranger for the smallest park in the National Park System sounds like a pretty good job. And the Thaddeus Kosciuszko National Memorial in Philadelphia is only .02 acres in size, so you just have to take a few steps to get from one side of it to the other. This makes it easy to spot vagrants trying to camp illegally at the memorial, which is basically a small messy room where Thaddeus Kosciuszko lived for seven months.

"But who's Thaddeus Kosciuszko?" you ask. Surely you jest! Thomas Jefferson called Kosciuszko "the purest son of liberty I have ever known." He was the most famous Polish hero of the American Revolutionary War, serving as the head engineer for the Continental Army.

Upon later returning to Poland, Kosciuszko went on to lead the Polish army to several brilliant victories against an invading

Russian force. Although he never lost a battle, Kosciuszko lost the war when the Polish king surrendered in 1792.

So he's sort of like the Polish George Washington . . . if Washington had lost.

In 1797, Kosciuszko traveled to Philadelphia to try to get some back pay that was owed him. And our modern National Memorial is where he stayed for seven months before moving back to Europe.

Hang on, but excuse me sir, there's NO CAMPING here.

So That's Why His Signature is So Big!

Declaration of Independence signer John Hancock kept a full bowl of rum punch by his bedside at all hours.

THE DECLARATION OF INDEPENDENCE AND THE CONSTITUTION

The Declaration of Independence is short and easy to understand. A lot of it contains gripes about King George III, such as how he "destroyed the lives of our people." By the way, there is a famous story that the entry in the king's diary for July 4, 1776, reads, "Nothing of importance happened today." That's not true, so the next time you hear it, cry out, "Poppycock! King George never kept a diary."

The movie *National Treasure* revealed that the Declaration of Independence is actually a treasure map with secret codes! Oh, wait, was it the Constitution? Now I forget!

Americans often get the Declaration and the Constitution mixed up. They say things like, "Don't mess with my constitutional right to life, liberty, and the pursuit of happiness." Ha! There isn't any such thing.

To clear it up, the Declaration of Independence came first, in 1776, and the Constitution was written eleven years later. The Declaration mentions the phrase "life,

Sideline Rebels

Of the fifty-six men who signed the Declaration of Independence, many took no part in the Revolutionary War. Of those who did participate in the war effort, only one was shot: Button Gwinnett, who died in a duel with a fellow American in 1777.

liberty, and the pursuit of happiness," as well as "all men are created equal."

Although it's a brilliantly important document, some people have found the Declaration's writing to be second-rate. In 1856, the renowned lawyer/politician Rufus Choate criticized its "glittering generalities." To this, writer Ralph Waldo Emerson answered, "Glittering generalities!? They are blazing ubiquities." (Oh, *snap*.)

Historically, the Declaration served the function of a Revolutionary coach giving a good pep talk to his soldiers. And the pep talk worked. As the new American government started, there were high hopes. The United States could win the war, cut its ties to England, and life would be good!

But life *wasn't* good. American citizens started suing each other, quarreling, and giving out more knickerbocker wedgies than they ever had before. John Quincy Adams wrote that the country was groaning under its "accumulated evils," and one politician even wrote to Prince Henry of Prussia to see if he'd be interested in providing some much-needed leadership. (He wasn't.)

To address the problem, a group of men locked themselves in a really hot room in Philadelphia, where they hammered out a series of laws. It was a difficult process, involving a lot of debate and even some unpleasant words.

JAMES MADISON: I'D LIKE TO MAKE ONE MORE OBSERVATION.

ALEXANDER HAMILTON: IF YOU'RE GOING TO KEEP MAKING OBSERVATIONS, MAYBE WE SHOULD BUILD A DOME OVER YOU AND STICK A TELESCOPE IN YOUR —

JAMES MADISON: I GET THE IDEA.

If the Declaration of Independence was the pregame pep talk, the Constitution was a brilliant new game plan created during a time-out. The beauty of the Constitution is that it cleverly deals with the fact that we, the people, can be selfish and power hungry.

Today, the United States Constitution is both the *shortest* (at twenty-five pages) and the *oldest* constitution of any country, and it's inspired brilliance across the world. But, oh, is it *tricky*. While Woodrow Wilson called it "too complex to be understood," a genius has figured out the Constitution's basic principles for you:

★It's hard to change the government unless enough people support the change.

★Power will be spread around so that a few people can't oppress everyone else. (These *checks* and *balances* explain why knickerbocker wedgies have been extinct for centuries.)

★Compromise is encouraged.

Not bad! While Alexander Hamilton

Sometimes a Great Notion

At the Constitutional Convention, a proposal was made that the United States army should be restricted to five thousand soldiers. George Washington reportedly said that this was fine, as long as the proposal also prohibited enemy armies from invading with more than *three thousand* men!

called the Constitution "a weak and worthless fabric," at least it's a fabric that can be altered to better fit the nation as it grows. Thomas Jefferson wrote, "Some men look at constitutions with sanctimonious reverence, and deem them . . . too sacred to touch. They ascribe to the [Founding Fathers] a wisdom more than human." Jefferson couldn't stand the thought of this. The whole *idea* was that the Founding Fathers did the best they could, but future generations might be able to do better.

What Would the Founding Fathers Do?

People often pretend to know what the Founding Fathers would do. You know, like "the Founding Fathers NEVER intended for the Constitution to be used for a paper airplane," that sort of thing.

Luckily, the Founding Fathers were brilliant enough to see this coming. John Adams wrote to a younger admirer, "I ought not object to your reverence for your fathers, but to tell you a very great secret ... I have no reason to believe that we were better than you are."

To answer the question "What would the Founding Fathers do?" Thomas Jefferson wrote, "This they would say themselves, were they to rise from the grave. ... Laws and institutions must go hand in hand with the progress of the human mind." And Jefferson was absolutely against "the dead hand of the past" being used to make decisions.

In other words, as people change for the better, so must their nation. *Booyah!* So the next time you hear a sentence start with "If our Founding Fathers were alive today . . ." remember that it's baloney, no matter how you slice it.

As scholar Belva Scroggins said, "Only wussies fear changing the Constitution." (Scroggins was a little-known historical figure. In fact, she's so obscure, she didn't actually exist.)

Over the two centuries of its history, the Constitution has been successfully changed or "amended" twenty-seven times.[3] These amendments have done helpful things like giving women the right to vote and allowing your neighbors to stockpile assault rifles.

3. *The first ten of those amendments are called the Bill of Rights, and they are usually considered to be part of the original document.*

Hey, I Memorized the Pledge of Allegiance!

In 1937, a man named Harry Wilhelm went to Washington, D.C., and recited the entire Constitution from *memory*. (What a suck-up!) It took him two hours.

LET'S LEARN MORE!

Though an armed revolution created the United States, today's American citizens seeking to revolutionize society are encouraged to initiate and pass constitutional amendments. There have been about ten thousand of these proposed amendments over the years. Most fail. One of my favorite failures was an amendment to change the USA to the USE: the *United States of Earth*.

See if you can tell the *real* failed constitutional amendments from the *fake* ones.

96

(Answers below.[4])

A. SAME-SEX MARRIAGES WILL BE OUTLAWED.

B. ALL ACTS OF WAR SHALL BE PUT TO A NATIONAL VOTE.
ANYONE VOTING FOR WAR SHALL BE REGISTERED AS
A VOLUNTEER FOR SERVICE IN THE UNITED STATES
ARMED FORCES.

C. THE PRESIDENT SHALL BE REPLACED BY A "COUNCIL
OF THREE."

D. DRUM SOLOS AT ROCK CONCERTS WILL BE LIMITED
TO TWO MINUTES.

E. ALL CITIZENS HAVE THE RIGHT TO LIVE IN AN UNPOL-
LUTED ENVIRONMENT.

F. THE ARMY AND NAVY SHALL BE ABOLISHED.

---

4.   They're all real except for D.

How to Win an Election

"WE ALWAYS WANT THE BEST MAN TO WIN AN ELECTION. UNFORTUNATELY, HE NEVER RUNS." —Will Rogers

Running for office has never been easy. A good candidate needs a brilliant mind along with a strong stomach and thick skin. How bad can it get? Well, when Andrew Jackson ran for president in 1828, his opponents called his mother a prostitute. Worse, they also said that Jackson was bad at "orthography." *Those jerks!*

To get an idea of how tough it can be to

go up for election, imagine you had to run for office to be *you*. In other words, you wouldn't get to exist unless enough people *voted* for you to exist. Would you get elected?

Keep in mind that *any* stupid things you've said or done will be used against you, and even shown on YouTube. If you're anything like me, you'd be in constant "damage control" mode, trying to convince people that you aren't a meanie, nitwit, or member of the Whig Party.

Exactly who would be willing to go through all that trouble? This question should give you an insight into how needy, power hungry, or (gasp!) idealistic someone would have to be to voluntarily run for office.

If you ever decide to throw your diaper into the ring to be student body treasurer, state senator, or just yourself, you'll need a few pointers drawn from history. Sure, you're brilliant, but every little bit helps.

Americans Get More Exercise

While an American candidate "runs" for election, a French candidate "presents" himself or herself for office. And in England, interested folks "stand" for election. How hard could that be?

★ Hire a hatchet man and some henchmen to take care of your legwork. (Henchmen love legwork!) That way, if any of your dirty tricks backfire, you can blame them. Then you can fire them. Finally, you can hire them back when no one is looking.

★ Research your opponent's background. Use a thesaurus to find fancy synonyms describing his or her life story. Give speeches using these words in a snotty way.

When George Smathers ran against Claude Pepper in Florida in 1950, Smathers snarled that his opponent was a "homo sapiens" who had "matriculated"

100

and "engaged in celibacy." Worse, Claude was "a known extrovert" whose sister was a "thespian."[1]

The voters were horrified! (And Smathers won the election.)

★ Find a symbol that makes you look good, regardless of whether it's appropriate.

When running for president, William Henry Harrison used the image of a log cabin to represent himself as a "man of the people." This "man of the people" routine was at odds with the fact that Harrison lived in a mansion located on two thousand acres of land and that his father was a signer of the Declaration of Independence.

The log cabin image worked so well, Harrison campaigned from a portable

---

1. *Meaning that Claude Pepper was a human who had graduated from school and who had not had sex before marrying. Worse, he was outgoing and his sister was an actress.*

log cabin that was built on a wagon bed. Yep, log cabins had a lot of power in early American politics. Both Abraham Lincoln and Confederate States of America president Jefferson Davis were born in log cabins. And Senator Daniel Webster once apologized to a crowd for *not* being born in one!

★ Learn the trick called the Irish Switch. This is the move where a politician shakes hands with one person, talks to a second voter, and smiles at a third voter all at once.

102

John F. Kennedy was so good at the Irish Switch, he once reportedly foiled a pickpocket by unexpectedly shaking the thief's hand.

Other public appearance tips: Learn the person's first name and use it. Also, lean toward voters when you speak to them. Oh, and promise them anything they want. Voters like that. They're smart enough to know not to take a candidate's promises seriously.

★ Show up for at least one campaign event dressed in a white toga. Explain to people that it's a "toga candida," the traditional outfit for Romans running for office.

Log Cabin Libations

To cash in on log cabin fever, a distiller named E. C. Booz began selling log-cabin-shaped whiskey bottles known as "Old Cabin Whiskey." "Booze" eventually became a slang word for hard liquor.

★ Accuse your opponent of being bankrupt and of having gone through an ugly divorce. Even if this isn't true, you can say that he or she is "morally bankrupt" and "divorced from reality." (This will work especially well in middle school and high school elections.)

★ If you end up debating your opponent, be sure to say, "I could not fail to disagree with you less" if you agree with him. (Another option: say "I non-concur" if you disagree.)

Chicken Ducks Debate

In 1972, John Lindsay was running in the presidential primaries against George Wallace. Since Wallace refused to debate, Lindsay's supporters released eight chickens in a crowd listening to Wallace speak.

Each chicken had a sign that read, "I'm George Wallace and I'm afraid to debate."

In the following confusion, you can simply declare yourself the winner!

All in the Family

In 1932, future three-term governor of Louisiana Earl Long called his political enemy, Huey Long, a "son of a b****." The problem was that Earl and Huey were *brothers!*

★ Hire a stenographer to hang around your opponent and take notes on what he or she says. Then creatively edit these statements to give them a sinister new meaning.

That way something like "My mom told me a story about George Wallace and a chicken that is a real killer" becomes "My mom . . . is a real killer."

★ If your opponent is heavily favored, legally change your name so that it's the same as your opponent.

105

Robert Casey lost two elections in Pennsylvania when the opposing party confused voters by running *another* Robert Casey against him. Casey finally won an election in 1987 and served as governor for the next eight years.

Bad Education

No one ever graduates from Electoral College. It's not a school, but rather the group of people whose votes decide the election of the president. When you cast a vote for president, you're NOT voting for the president—you're voting for Electoral College delegates who have kind of, sort of promised to vote for your candidate. And that's why it's the worst college in America!

Thomas Jefferson called the Electoral College "the most dangerous blot in our Constitution." Yet despite about seven hundred congressional attempts at improvements, it hasn't really changed for two centuries.

Have You Heard of "In a Pig's Eye"?

Nastiness has long been a part of political campaigns. When Grover Cleveland ran for president, his opponents gave out small toy pigs. If you looked up the pig's butt, you saw Cleveland's face!

★ Don't try to buy votes. It can get expensive. In 1910, an investigation into an Ohio vote-buying scandal convicted 1,500 men of selling their votes for an average of $8. (Hmmm, even though that would be a lot more in today's money, maybe it's not so expensive after all.)

107

To get out of actually *paying* for a vote, election campaigns used to regularly hold alcohol-fueled parties for voters. Heck, even George Washington plied his voters with drink to sway their political inclinations.

This was such a widespread practice that in 1792 a newspaper wrote, "The voice of the people is the voice of grog." (Grog is liquor mixed with water.)

★ Be careful about who endorses you.

In 1898, Teddy Roosevelt was running for the governor's office in New York. As this was right after the Spanish-American War, Teddy had one of the former sergeants in his command speak for him. He was a man named Buck Taylor, and he said:

[TEDDY] KEPT EVERY PROMISE HE MADE TO US, AND HE WILL TO YOU. . . . HE TOLD US . . . WE WOULD HAVE TO LIE OUT IN THE TRENCHES WITH THE RIFLE BULLETS CLIMBING OVER US. . . . HE TOLD US WE MIGHT MEET WOUNDS AND DEATH . . . HE LED US UP SAN JUAN HILL LIKE SHEEP TO THE SLAUGHTER AND SO HE WILL LEAD YOU.

Not helpful.

★ Don't stuff the ballot box. It's wrong, and if you win, you'll always feel guilty about it. Take Charles D. B. King of Liberia, for example. Liberia is a West African country begun by freed American slaves in 1820. In 1923, Charles D. B. King ran for president and won with more than 240,000 votes.

This was overkill, since there were only 15,000 registered voters in the entire country. And I'm sure Mr. King always felt bad about that.

109

★ Do not physically attack your opponent.

In 1998, a man named Byron Looper decided to run for state senator. First, he legally changed his name to Byron "Low Tax" Looper. Then, to assure himself of victory, he murdered his opponent just before election day. Though Looper denied committing the crime, a friend of his testified that Looper had said, "I did it! I killed that guy I was running against!"

★ NEVER insult your voters. Senator Jim Watson once said, "You can vote for me or go to hell." (Hearing of this, Calvin Coolidge said, "He gave them a difficult alternative.")

Watson lost the election.

HONING YOUR SKILLS

The ability to think on your feet will be important to you as you run for office. Between the interviews, the debates, and the hecklers ("Mom, PLEASE stop embarrassing me!"), you need to be able to get off a good line quickly.

Study some of the masters of this art. For example, in 1928, presidential candidate Al Smith was at a campaign stop when a heckler yelled, "Go ahead, Al, don't let me bother you. Tell 'em all you know. It won't take long."

Smith shot back, "If I tell them all we *both* know, it won't take any longer." The crowd *ooh-ed* and *aah-ed*!

Another sensei of the quick quip was Senator Fritz Hollings. During a television debate in 1986, his opponent challenged him to take a drug test.

"I'll take a drug test," Hollings shot back, "if you'll take an IQ test." Now *that's* brilliance!

Wanna Be a Cowboy?

> "BY 1890, THE WEST HAD BEEN TAMED AND COULD EVEN OBEY SIMPLE COMMANDS SUCH AS 'SIT!'"
> —Dave Barry

Imagine America's frontier expanding westward. Perhaps you picture pioneers building log cabins across the nation. Wait, you're not picturing log cabins in the desert, are you? Sure, you could build a cactus cabin, but the screams might attract coyotes.

Never before in history has a nation grown as large and as quickly as the United States. While Canada and Russia are larger, neither country has anything close to America's geographic diversity. With extensive coastlines on both the Atlantic and the Pacific, America had the challenge of getting people to occupy all the territory in between.

So how's this for a deal: after paying $18 for an application, you get 160 acres of land. The condition is that you have to build a house on the land and then live there for five years.

Sound good? You betcha! Starting in 1862, the Homestead Act gave away 270 million acres of federal land in the west to homesteaders. By 1890, the frontier was officially declared "closed."

Of course, homesteaders had to make their own way to the land they wanted. Our ability to Google-map destinations makes it hard to imagine what a roadless country the United States once was. And I don't mean *before* settlers moved into an area, I mean AFTER! In the mid-1700s, roads were so nonexistent, most people in the colonies had never even seen a wagon, much less a carriage. Without roads, there was no point in having one! (In 1750, the whole state of Massachusetts only had six carriages.)

Not that you'd want to ride in one of those old-school carriages anyway. Shock-absorbing springs didn't get added to them until the early 1800s, which is why one popular carriage route was called the Shake Gut Line. The BEST way to travel was often on a "corduroy road," which was made of tree trunks laid crossways across the roadway. My guts are shaking just imagining that . . . though it's possible that I overdid it with the granola this morning.

Thank goodness railroads came along. Beginning in about 1830, you could ride along in a railcar that was attached to

"Whoa...Oops!"

In 1867, an average of four New York pedestrians were killed each week by horses. That's slightly more than the city's weekly traffic fatalities today.

the other cars by a very safe chain. If all the cigar smoking made the car too stuffy, you could open the window and have hot cinders blow into your face from the coal-burning engine!

Well into the twentieth century, "highways" were what we might call bad roads. "Roads" were trails, and "trails" were sometimes invisible pathways. In 1905, there still wasn't even *one mile* of paved rural highway in the whole nation.

To give you an idea of how bad the roads were, in 1919, West Point graduate Dwight "Ike" Eisenhower left Washington, D.C., as part of a transcontinental army convoy across the United States. The trip was over three thousand miles long and took sixty-two days.

And that set a new speed record for a transcontinental road trip across North America!

But as the number of cars increased, drivers got frustrated at having to drive on few and crummy roads. With the government lagging on road construction, the first road across the United States (and the first transcontinental highway in the world) was built using *private* donations. Amazing! Called the Lincoln Highway (aka US Route 30), it opened in 1923. Upon seeing the Lincoln's success and usefulness, the federal government almost reluctantly began funding other interstate highways.

When former convoy member Dwight Eisenhower became president, he authorized the construction of more than forty thousand miles of national superhighways in 1956. Cars poured out of factories and onto the roads as never before. There was an environmental and safety cost to this; as Ralph Nader wrote in 1965, "the automobile has brought death, injury, and the most inestimable sorrow and deprivation to millions of people."

Meanwhile, the idea of mass transit (e.g., subways, buses, light rail) was very nearly forgotten. Less than 1 percent of the federal transportation was given to mass transit in 1956. That amount has increased to a not-very-whopping 13 percent today. (It's almost enough to make me want to build a cactus log cabin.)

117

CANADA: WATCHING, LEARNING . . . WAITING?

Americans fought a Revolutionary War for independence and then expanded their country westward, messily demolishing Indian cultures as they went. To the north, Canadians watched. After fending off United States aggression in the War of 1812, they continued to watch the American example, and then pursued a very different path to liberty.

Canadians achieved independence through a series of cordial meetings with the British. *Bor-ring!* But despite

It Is Your Destiny

In 1845, a New York newspaperman invented the term "manifest destiny." His idea was that God had chosen America to take over and populate the entire North American continent.

the Canadians' most diplomatic efforts, there was bound to be some friction with the United States. The result: the Aroostook War. This forgotten battle raged between Canada and the United States from 1838–39.

TOTAL AMERICAN CASUALTIES: one cow injured, along with a few militiamen.

TOTAL CANADIAN CASUALTIES: one injured pig.

As for Canada's "Wild West," please! One of Canada's bloodiest events from those years may be the Cypress Hills Massacre. In 1873, American whiskey traders crossed the border and killed more than a hundred members of the Assiniboine tribe for "stealing horses." It later turned out that their horses had actually been taken by *Cree* Indians.

That means Americans caused Canada's worst travesty! The Royal Canadian Mounted Police was established that very year to prevent future lawlessness.

The worst problems the Mounties faced continued to be Americans illegally crossing the border to peddle liquor or other forms of trouble to the Indians.

Canadians never understood the hatred some Americans had for Indians. One Mountie wrote in wonderment, "These men always look upon the Indians as their natural enemy." As for Indians, they came to speak of the border between Canada and the United States as the

Foul Language for Meriwether

Explorers Lewis and Clark get a lot of ink for crossing North America between 1804 and 1806. But the two learned they weren't the first English speakers to travel their route when an Indian in the Pacific Northwest greeted them with repeated calls of "*son-of-a-pitch!*" He had apparently heard trappers say this so frequently, he'd assumed it was a standard greeting for whites.

"medicine line." To the north, freedom. To the south, danger.

O PIONEERS!

Close your eyes and imagine that you have fallen into a time machine (they're everywhere!) and are transported back in time to 1845. Hmmm, if your eyes are closed, you can't read what I'm writing. Okay, open your eyes, but *keep* imagining! You're in a covered wagon, and as you lift the canvas to look outside, you see that your wagon is part of a wagon train. Looks like you're on the Oregon Trail. Wow!

Suddenly, you hear Indians whooping. They sure sound angry! "Circle the wagons!" you shout at the other covered wagons.

Because of your futuristic hairstyle and air of authority, the wagon leaders listen to you. And so they begin the incredibly slow process of bringing all the wagons around to form a defensive circle. But

121

this takes so long, everyone is killed by arrows and fragment grenades before the wagons have even formed a curve.

Man, you must have really bad luck. The odds of a Great Plains pioneer dying in a battle with Indians in the mid-1800s was .001 percent!

122

As you survey the damage, a man with an arrow piercing his handlebar mustache staggers to you. He utters, "Thanks for the help," and then pitches facedown into the dirt.

Okay, you can stop imagining. I'm sorry to have to teach you such a harsh lesson, but circling the wagons would never have worked. So don't try it, even in your imagination.

"THE MUTILATION," OR, THE MULLET THAT ROARED

The Mutilation is the name used south of the United States–Mexico border for the Mexican War (1846–48). Though you

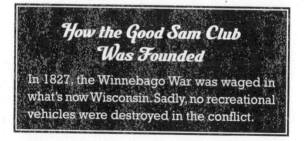

How the Good Sam Club Was Founded

In 1827, the Winnebago War was waged in what's now Wisconsin. Sadly, no recreational vehicles were destroyed in the conflict.

123

may have forgotten about it, rest assured that Mexico hasn't.

The American president at that time was James Polk, an innovator of the haircut now known as the "mullet." Polk's mullet superpowers—and a little thing called the United States Army—enabled him to take Texas, California, and Colorado from Mexico. But it was an odd operation all the way around. Initially, Polk offered Mexico $25 million for California, a deal that Mexico refused.

Next, Polk made a case for war against Mexico, claiming that Mexico's troops "had shed American blood upon American soil." An Illinois congressman named

Tempting!

To get Mexico to enter World War I on its side, Germany promised to give back Arizona, New Mexico, and Texas if the United States was defeated.

Abraham Lincoln asked if he could see the spot where that bloody soil was, but he (and his vote against the Mexican War) were ignored. The Mexican War was on, and American troops marched all the way to Mexico City in fairly short order.

Without any other choice, the Mexican government agreed to sell about half of its entire territory to the United States for $15 million in early 1848.

But *La Mutilación* was not quite done. Six years later, Mexico sold what is now New Mexico and Arizona to the United States for another $10 million. Even though that's a big parcel, the sale could have been for a *much* bigger area. The original property included nearly all of Mexico's current northernmost states and ALL of Baja California. But that deal stalled in Congress from fear of increasing the South's power and size.

Before leaving office, Polk and his mullet also settled the border disputes in the

Pacific Northwest, which led to statehood for Oregon and Washington shortly thereafter.

You know what they say about mullets: business in the front, territorial expansion in the back.

COWBOYS!

When asked what type of historical American figure he'd like to be, the average man answers, "Wild West cowboy."

But just because cowpokes were out on the open range, raising cattle, raising heck, and spitting tobaccy juice, don't think everything was that great. Even though cowboys were herding grade-A beef, they often had to eat meat that tasted like possum after a bad divorce. (I'm not sure what that means, but I like the sound of it.)

In fact, cowboys were apparently the inventors of the dish known as "son-of-a-b****

stew." This was a dish made from meat that was so vile, the only possible thing you could say after tasting it was "son of a b****." (Now *that* will make you upchuck by the chuck wagon!)

The upchucking didn't last very long, though. The era of real cowboys going on long cattle drives took place for only about twenty years between the 1860s and

1880s. Even in their heyday (hayday?), there were never more than about ten thousand cowboys at any one time. That means farmers outnumbered cowboys by about one thousand to one. *Humph*!

THE WORST SENTENCE EVER

If you've made it this far, you've already read some really bad sentences. But let me refer for a moment to sentences pronounced in a court of law. While lots

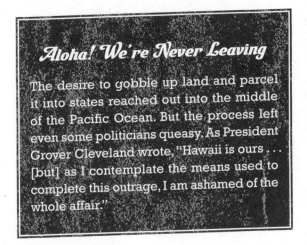

Aloha! We're Never Leaving

The desire to gobble up land and parcel it into states reached out into the middle of the Pacific Ocean. But the process left even some politicians queasy. As President Grover Cleveland wrote, "Hawaii is ours . . . [but] as I contemplate the means used to complete this outrage, I am ashamed of the whole affair."

of cutthroats and ne'er-do-wells were hanged in the Wild West days, Judge Isaac Parker gave his death sentences more gusto than his colleagues on the bench. For example, the "Hanging Judge" once sentenced a man to death for murder like this:

[I command that you] hang until you are dead, dead, dead. And . . . further that such officer or officers retire quietly from your swinging, dangling corpse, that the vultures may descend upon your filthy body and pick the putrid flesh therefrom till nothing remains but the bare, bleached bones of a cold-blooded . . . bloodthirsty . . . guilty, sheep-herding . . . son-of-a-b****.

Wait, I don't get it. Was this guy found guilty or innocent?

129

WRITING PROMPT

It's a given that American frontiers-people had more guts and brains than most Americans do today. These stalwart men and women were unafraid to take on huge challenges and then survive by virtue of their wits and resourcefulness.

Sadly, modern life doesn't give us many opportunities to look death in the eye and then build a log cabin. But I am about to provide you with such an opportunity: write the history of the United States as a series of limericks. Avoid referring to people from Nantucket anywhere in your work. Good luck and Godspeed.

Dance Fever

Choreograph an interpretive dance that pays homage to the Winnebago War. (Try to work in James Polk's mullet if at all possible.) Reward your audience after the show by serving bowls of son-of-a- b**** stew.

Playin' It Old School

"GAMES . . . STAMP NO CHARACTER ON THE MIND."—*Thomas Jefferson*

The exciting game of anvil shooting dates back to the Revolutionary War. American soldiers started the tradition of firing their guns into the air during Fourth of July celebrations, and next thing you knew, they got more ambitious. After all, why shoot a gun when you can launch an anvil?

131

THE RULES:

FIRST, get one large anvil.

THEN, get another large anvil.

FINALLY, obtain a lot of high-grade gunpowder. Then take your items to an open field. Place one anvil on the ground, upside down. Fill the opening (anvils have cavities on the bottom) with gunpowder. Now run a long fuse out of the cavity.

NEXT, put the second anvil on top of the first one. Now light the fuse! Enjoy the

132

subsequent explosion, and be sure to keep your eyes on the top anvil. If you followed the directions, it should be somersaulting up over a hundred feet in the air!

The most important part of the game is making sure you don't get touched by the anvil on its descent.

After the Civil War, there was an influx of affordable Chinese firecrackers into the United States. This helped make shooting the anvil increasingly rare. At the same time, various competitive sports began

Your Doll Looks Like My Grandma!

The idea of a girl playing with a doll that's about her own age is a fairly new one. Throughout history, there weren't many toys for girls, and if a girl did get a doll, it was usually a doll that looked like an *adult*, not a baby or young girl.

133

to take center stage. Some of these were popular enough to transfix an entire state, like football in Texas, basketball in Indiana, or bocce ball in Oregon.

Another Civil War favorite was "one o'cat." The game was set up with a home plate and one other base. The player at bat scored runs by getting a hit and then running to the base and back home without getting out.

While waiting for the next battle, soldiers in camp had the opportunity to share games from their own regions. One favorite was "town ball." It was like baseball, except there were no foul balls,

Stickball Diplomacy

The Choctaw Indians were so devoted to stickball, the results of stickball games were used to settle disputes between towns.

and the runners could be gotten "out" by throwing the ball at them!

As for baseball, it had been around since the 1830s. Although it was very similar to today's game, as late as the 1860s, players wore no gloves and the pitching was underhand. It was over the next twenty years that players started wearing gloves (they weren't nearly as big as today's mitts) and pitchers were burning it in overhand.

By the twentieth century, baseball spawned one of the greatest American sports figures ever, George "Babe" Ruth. The chubby American became so famous worldwide, Japanese soldiers in World War II often cried, "To hell with Babe Ruth!" as they attacked.

Historians have analyzed vintage base-ball games from Babe Ruth's time and concluded that there are some differences between the old days of baseball and modern baseball: the athletes of former eras didn't trash talk, chest bump, hot dog, high-five, point to the sky, butt pat, or kiss jewelry. Other than that, it's pretty much the same.

For decades, baseball was the king of American sports. Historian Jacques Barzun even wrote, "To understand the heart of America, one must know baseball." But while baseball still does quite nicely, it no longer captures the soul of the

"Take me out to the— hey, this game sucks!"

In 1908, a man named Jack Norworth and a friend wrote a song called "Take Me Out to the Ball Game." As you know, it's now sung at all professional baseball games in the United States. But Jack Norworth had never actually *been* to a baseball game before he wrote his song. When Norworth finally did go to one, many years later, he wasn't very impressed.

nation. Hey, it's the twenty-first century! We've moved on to a love affair with full-contact sports, like mixed martial arts ballroom dancing.

Another full-contact sport with an all-American pedigree is football. But it got off to a slow start. In its early years, football was thought of by many as barbaric. Games were often bloody brawls that the spectators sometimes joined. The carnage at Army-Navy games was especially intense, and the rivalry was cancelled for four years in the 1890s after a general slapped an admiral! ("Damn your torpedoes!")

In 1905 alone, there were more than thirty fatalities from football, most of them stemming from the thinly padded helmets worn by the players. Teddy Roosevelt rescued the game from roughness by ordering the creation of a group to make and enforce rules for college players: the NCAA.

The NCAA helped make the game safer and more sportsmanlike. Since 1935, the Heisman Trophy has been given to the most outstanding NCAA football player. It's named for John Heisman, one-time football coach at Georgia Tech. How good a sport was he? Well, in 1916, he coached his team to a halftime score of 126–0 over Cumberland College. At the break, he warned his team not to let up, "Because you never know what those Cumberland players have up their sleeves."

Right. The game's final score was 222–0, and Heisman had earned the nickname "Ole Shut the Gates of Mercy."

DIGGING DEEPER

Many hip-hop artists are devoted chess players. Surprised? Don't be! Hip-hop and chess are actually quite similar. As Wu-Tang Clan founder RZA said, "Hip-hop is a battle game. Chess is a battle."[1]

This has paved the way for the thinking man's version of combat and strategy: *Hip-Hop Chess.* This mix of chess-playing with music also includes the study of martial arts like jujitsu. It's designed to help young people focus their minds and

---

1. *Jay Z raps in "This Life Forever": "Over my years I've seen Rooks get tooken by the Knight / Lose they crown by tryna defend a Queen / Checkmate, in four moves the Bobby Fischer of rap."*

to cultivate their brilliance. (Think of it as an intellectual's fight club.)

In addition to playing Hip-Hop Chess, consider other combinations of music and games where you can get to "flexin' your mentals." To get started, some ideas include:

BEBOP BACKGAMMON

HEAVY METAL TIDDLYWINKS

MARIACHI MAH-JONG

ZYDECO DOMINOES

Brilliant Women

"HISTORY IS NOT THE PROVINCE OF THE LADIES." —*John Adams*

"REMEMBER ALL MEN WOULD BE TYRANTS IF THEY COULD." —*Abigail Adams*

In 1848, a group of women gathered in Seneca Falls, New York, to do something brilliant. (No, this wasn't a meeting of the Red Hat Society.) Together, these women wrote something called the Declaration of Sentiments, which was composed by rewriting sections of the Declaration of Independence.

For example, the second paragraph of the Declaration of Sentiments starts, "We hold these truths to be self-evident: that all men and *women* are created equal—"

Did you see that? The women inserted the words "and WOMEN" into the sentence. Brilliant! And they weren't done, either. Compare these two passages:

Declaration of Independence	*Declaration of Sentiments*
The history of the present King of Great Britain is a history of repeated injuries ... [in] establishment of an absolute Tyranny over these States.	*The history of mankind is a history of repeated injuries ... on the part of man toward woman ... [in] establishment of an absolute Tyranny over her.*

Sentimental Journey

Charlotte Woodward was the only woman to attend the 1848 Seneca Falls Convention who lived to see the day when all women could vote. But she was too ill on Election Day 1920 to travel to a polling place!

At the time, these women were known as Feminists. Many men and women considered this a downright perplexing thing to be. Since not everyone understood what a Feminist was, writer Alice Miller helpfully defined it in a poem:

"MOTHER, WHAT IS A FEMINIST?"

"A FEMINIST, MY DAUGHTER,

IS ANY WOMAN NOW WHO CARES

TO THINK ABOUT HER OWN AFFAIRS

AS MEN DON'T THINK SHE OUGHTER."

Feminism had to be created because Masculinists had been running civilization for a very long time, and they hadn't always done a very good job of it. Not only were women in the United States not allowed to vote, they were also discouraged from even being *funny*. As one idiotic bit of American advice went:

"THOUGH YOU'RE BRIGHT AND THOUGH YOU'RE PRETTY, THEY'LL NOT LOVE YOU IF YOU'RE WITTY."

Another bit of rhyme pointed out the difficulty women had in getting recognition for their accomplishments, however modest:

IF WHAT I DO PROVE WELL, IT WON'T ADVANCE

THEY'LL SAY IT'S STOLEN OR ELSE IT WAS BY CHANCE.

—*Anne Bradstreet, 1650*

So let's see, women couldn't vote, own property, or be funny . . . what else? Oh yes, education was out as well. An education might encourage girls in their own ambitions! And only a man was encouraged to make something of himself. (As a puffed-up fellow once boasted, "I'm a self-made man." A nearby woman quipped, "God is pleased not to be responsible.") One 1773 manual for women warned, "If you happen to have any learning, keep it a profound secret, especially from the men." Why keep it secret? Because for a woman to make a "good wife," an education would be a liability.

So, for hundreds of years, women had their mental growth stunted. Their natural curiosity, ambition, and talent were mere distractions from the important stuff: childbearing and doing chores. In 1790, the average American mother lived to be forty years old (!) and had around a half-dozen children to tend to. Who knows how many female geniuses wasted away in the kitchen or out on the farm?

But drunks and alcoholics helped to change all that! After the Civil War, hard-drinking veterans motivated more and more women, especially in the Midwest, to band together against liquor. It was an odd time in United States history; while women couldn't vote, they did have freedom of speech. By lobbying, parading, and petitioning, they succeeded in outlawing liquor sales in some areas of the country. Women were learning to find creative ways to make a political difference.

Kate Warne: Private Eye

In 1861, Abraham Lincoln was informed of a plot to assassinate him while he traveled. To foil the plot, Lincoln changed his travel schedule and posed as an invalid being accompanied by his "sister." This part was played by Kate Warne, now known as America's first female private detective. (Warne had been working for the Pinkerton detective agency for five years before this assignment.)

FROM SLAVERY TO THE SUPREME COURT

Lucy Prince composed the first-known poetry written by an African American. She was born in West Africa, where she was kidnapped and brought to New England. In her early twenties, Prince witnessed an Indian raid in Massachusetts in 1746. She described the raid in a poem, excerpted here:

EUNICE ALLEN SEEN THE INDIANS COMING

AND HOPED TO SAVE HERSELF BY RUNNING

AND HAD NOT HER PETTICOATS STOPPED HER,

THE AWFUL CREATURES HAD NOT CAUGHT HER,

NOR TOMMYHAWKED HER ON THE HEAD,

AND LEFT HER ON THE GROUND FOR DEAD.

Born as a slave, Lucy married a free black man in 1756. She had six children (Caesar, Durexa, Drucella, Festus, Tatnai, and Abijah) and made her mark as a woman who was unafraid to speak her mind. When her son Caesar was denied admission to Williams College on the basis of race, she argued his case before the college trustees for three hours. Although they still didn't admit Caesar, this may have been the first case of a black woman fighting publicly against discrimination. (As for Caesar, he went on to fight in the Revolutionary War.)

Lucy later argued a property claims case before the Vermont Supreme Court. The presiding judge said that Lucy "made a better argument than he had ever heard from a lawyer in Vermont."

BPFF! (BEST PIRATE FRIENDS FOREVER!)

Sailors have historically thought that having a woman on board is bad luck. But in the case of Anne Bonny, the pirates were happy to make an exception.

Born in 1698 to a wealthy plantation

family, Bonny was a rebellious girl who hooked up with a drifter. The two made their way to the Bahamas, where Bonny met colorful pirate "Calico Jack" Rackham. The two were a perfect match.

Well, maybe not *perfect*. When Calico Jack's pirates ransacked a Dutch merchant ship, a Dutch sailor was invited to join the pirates' crew. Bonny apparently had quite an eye for this Dutch sailor, which pleased Calico Jack so little, he was prepared to cut the Dutchman's throat.

And Calico Jack probably *would* have done so if the Dutchman hadn't opened his shirt revealing, uh, a female bosom! The sailor was actually Mary Read, a woman who had disguised herself as a

149

man in order to pursue a life at sea. "As you can see sir, I am no threat to you," Read supposedly said.

Oh, how they must have laughed! Bonny and Read became BPFF, joining in on subsequent raids during the next year. According to witness testimony, the two brandished guns and cutlasses, wailed like banshees, and cursed like, uh, sailor girls. The fun and games came to an end when a British navy ship caught up to Calico Jack's sloop and the pirate captain surrendered with only one shot fired.

Only *two* members of Calico Jack's crew fought the British: Bonny and Read! Shooting and slashing, the two hellcats were eventually subdued and taken prisoner along with the rest of the pirates.

Calico Jack was sentenced to death. "If you fought like a man, you wouldn't be hanged like a dog!" Bonny snarled at her former lover the day he was hanged. After his execution, Calico Jack's corpse was displayed in a large metal cage as a caution to other pirates.

As for Bonny and Read, they were also sentenced to death, but there was one little catch: they were both pregnant! In fact, after their sentences were read, they both informed the court that they were in a "pirate family" way. We know that Read died in prison, perhaps during childbirth, but Bonny's fate is unknown . . . she disappears from the historical record entirely.

EAVESDROPPER, AUTHOR, SEER

Mercy Otis Warren (1728–1814) is credited with being the anonymous author of the 1776 satire *The Blockheads*. She was America's first major female intellectual, and probably the first Feminist. Although Mercy had no formal schooling, she apparently picked up on things by spying on her brothers' tutors. If that's not a brilliant way to get the education denied to you, I don't know what is!

As an adult, Warren knew many of the Founding Fathers, and she lobbied that equal rights for women be included in the United States Constitution. No dice.

Most importantly, Warren could see the future. In 1805, she somehow knew that I'd be writing this book! She wrote that there would come a day when "corruption begins to prevail, when degeneracy marks the manners of the people, and weakens the sinews of the state . . . let some unborn historian, in a far distant day, detail the lapse, and hold up the contrast between a simple, virtuous, and free people, and a degenerate, servile race of beings, corrupted by wealth, effeminated by luxury, impoverished by licentiousness, and become the automatons of intoxicated ambition."

Ladies, gentleman, servile beings, and automatons, I am that "unborn historian." I mean, I *was,* back before I was born. Obviously, I'm born now. (This is confusing; am I a blockhead?)

THE SCOLDER ROYALL

Anne Newport Royall (1769–1854) was
the first professional female journalist
and a good watchdog. In order to get
President John Quincy Adams to answer
her questions, she followed him to the
Potomac River, where he liked to take
daily swims while naked. (Hail to the
Skinny-Dipping Chief!)

Royall sat on his clothes, refusing to budge
until the interview was completed.

Anne Royall didn't start off as a journalist.
As a young woman, she married Revolutionary War vet William Royall, but after
his death, a contested will and no pension
led her to earn a living by traveling the
United States and publishing accounts
of what she saw.

Royall was a canny researcher, and she
was able to uncover a plot in Philadelphia by a religious group looking to elect
candidates who could break down the

separation of church and state. Writing on this topic earned Royall a number of enemies. The polite ones burned her books, but one angry man pushed her down a staircase for being too snoopy.

Harassments followed, and Royall found herself routinely taunted and her home pelted with stones. When she complained to the authorities, she was stunned to find herself charged with being a "scold" and a disturber of the peace.

Outraged by this stupidity, Royall eventually began publishing newspapers committed to exposing sexist, corrupt, and lazy government bureaucrats. When she was offered a $2,000 bribe to keep quiet, it was front-page news on her own front page. And when some postmasters refused to deliver her paper to subscribers, she published their names in the newspaper as well!

Royall's newspaper ran for twenty-three years, until her death in 1854.

A PRIVATE PRIVATE

Private Robert Shurtlieff was slashed in the head and shot while fighting for the Continental Army. But what made him unique was that he was actually a *woman* named Deborah Sampson (1760–1827).

Sampson was a strapping farm girl who pulled her hair back and dressed in men's clothing to join the Revolution in the early 1780s. This was a laudable decision for two reasons: one, it showed she was a true patriot, and two, it allowed her to escape an arranged marriage with a lumpy local farmer.

Although she suffered wounds in battle, Sampson treated them herself so that she would not be found out. But after she caught a bad fever, an army doctor discovered the soldier's true gender. Sampson received an honorable discharge in 1783 and headed home to Massachusetts. There, her Baptist church expelled her from the congregation for enlisting as a soldier.

Sampson went on to marry a different, less lumpy farmer than the one she had run away from earlier. In 1802, she went on a speaking tour to share her experiences as the only known female soldier in the Revolutionary War. After her death in 1827, Sampson's family was the first in the United States to get a pension for military service performed by a woman.

During the Civil War, the need for soldiers on both sides was so great that army physicals were often no more than a firm handshake. As a result, more than four hundred women that we know of successfully masqueraded as men.

SECOND-CLASS-CITIZEN CAGE MATCH

Elizabeth Cady Stanton was a women's rights pioneer who went head-to-head in a battle royale with famous abolitionist and writer Frederick Douglass. During the Civil War, many suffragettes moved women's rights to the back burner to concentrate on emancipation for former slaves. But when Congress passed the Fourteenth Amendment in 1866 defining a citizen as "male," the women began to worry.

Their worry turned to outrage when, four years later, the Fifteenth Amendment gave the vote to black men while excluding women of all races. Stanton was a hard-core abolitionist, but when she learned of the constitutional amendment, she was steaming. In an 1869 debate with Douglass, Stanton said that the amendment would create an "aristocracy of sex on this continent," and wondered why men wanted an amendment that would "make their wives and mothers the political inferiors of unlettered and unwashed ditch-diggers, bootblacks, butchers, and barbers, fresh from the plantations of the South."

And she was just getting warmed up!

To this, Douglass responded, "When women, because they are women, are hunted down . . . when they are dragged from their homes and hung from lamp-posts; when their children are torn from their arms and their brains dashed out upon the pavement . . . then they will have an urgency to obtain the ballot equal to our own."

It's tough to argue with that.

VICTORY FOR VICTORIA!

The most fascinating woman to hail from Homer, Ohio, was Victoria Wood-hull (1838–1937).

Born to an eccentric family that had a medicine and fortune-telling show, Victoria and her sister Tennessee performed displays of hypnotism and spiritualism. The two sisters cut their hair short, dressed in men's clothing, and became as famous for their daring and style as they were for their psychic skills.

The two Woodhull sisters went to New York City in 1868, and word of their magnetic personalities spread. They continued their spiritual act, and through it they met the millionaire Cornelius Vanderbilt. The wealthy industrialist was interested in spirituality, and he gave the two sisters financial advice and support, which led to their creating the world's first female-owned stock brokerage, Woodhull, Claflin and Company. It was a success, and the two sisters became known as the "Queens of Finance."

In 1870, Victoria and Tennessee used their profits to start their own newspaper, *Woodhull and Claflin's Weekly*. It supported equal rights for women, short skirts, socialism, and legalized prostitution. And it opposed mustaches on men. (Really!)

If you think that's gutsy, that same year, Woodhull published the following:

"While others argued the equality of women with men, I proved it by successfully engaging in business; while others sought to show that there was no valid reason why women should be treated, socially and politically, as being inferior to men, I boldly entered the arena. . . . I now announce myself candidate for the Presidency."

Yep, Victoria Woodhull was the first female candidate for president! Her slogan was "Victory for Victoria." But despite (or because of) her bravery and determination, Woodhull suffered a torrent of abuse. Many men were intimidated or outraged by her, and even many women who agreed with her politics thought Woodhull had gone too far. Equal rights legend Susan B. Anthony supported Ulysses S. Grant, and *Harper's Weekly* cartoonist Thomas Nast labeled Woodhull as "Mrs. Satan."

Of course Woodhull lost, but if she had won, she *still* couldn't have been president. Woodhull would have been only

The Fix Is In

In 1940, comedian Gracie Allen ran for president on the Surprise Party ticket. To make fun of the very remote possibility of a woman being elected, her campaign slogan was, "It's in the bag."

thirty-four years old at her inauguration, and presidents have to be thirty-five!

In 1871, Woodhull had another first: she became the first woman to speak before a high congressional committee when she spoke out fiercely on women's rights to the House Judiciary Committee. With a modest demeanor, she proclaimed, "We are plotting revolution . . . we will overthrow this bogus Republic and plant a government of righteousness in its stead."

Ultimately, the Woodhull sisters became better known for their charitable contributions than for their politics. They took trips to Africa together, and upon Victoria's death, she was survived by her daughter: *Zulu Woodhull!*

WOMAN REBEL

In 1914, Margaret Sanger (1879–1966) published the newsletter *Woman Rebel* to inform women about a newfangled term she'd invented: "birth control." Sanger was

Voting the Feminine Way

The Nineteenth Amendment didn't allow women to vote until 1920, but states and territories had their own laws. In 1869, the governor of the Wyoming Territory approved a women's suffrage bill, and the next year, Louisa Swain became the first woman to vote in a United States election. The seventy-year-old housewife had to reassure reporters that voting had not made her any less of a woman.

trying to make birth control legal, safe, and acceptable. In the short run, it didn't work. She had to leave the United States to avoid arrest on obscenity charges. But upon returning, Sanger opened the nation's first birth-control clinic. *Then* she was arrested.

This was a deeply personal issue for Sanger. As a maternity nurse working in the ghettos of New York City, she saw

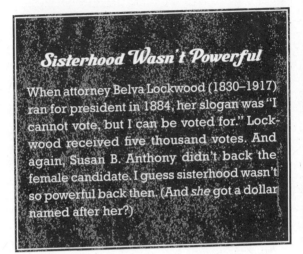

Sisterhood Wasn't Powerful

When attorney Belva Lockwood (1830–1917) ran for president in 1884, her slogan was "I cannot vote, but I can be voted for." Lockwood received five thousand votes. And again, Susan B. Anthony didn't back the female candidate. I guess sisterhood wasn't so powerful back then. (And *she* got a dollar named after her?)

firsthand the ways that unplanned pregnancies could destroy women's lives. Sanger's mother had eighteen pregnancies, with seven miscarriages among them, and died penniless at the age of fifty.

In the 1950s, Sanger and millionaire Katharine McCormick funded research that led to the invention of the birthcontrol pill. In 1960, "the pill" was approved by the Food and Drug Administration for birth-control use. Five years later, the Supreme Court struck down the anti-contraception laws that barred the pill's use in some areas. Sanger died shortly afterward.

SCHLEMIELS REJOICE!

With her gravelly Bronx accent, floppy hats, and cool name, equal rights champion Bella Abzug (1920–1998) was both memorable and powerful. Abzug was so boisterous, vice presidential candidate Geraldine Ferraro once said that Abzug "didn't knock lightly on the door. She didn't even push it open or batter it down. She took it off the hinges forever so that those of us who came after could walk through."

After becoming a lawyer specializing in civil rights, Abzug started wearing outrageous hats so that male lawyers would stop confusing her for a secretary. In the 1960s, she protested the Vietnam War.

In 1970, she ran for (and won) a seat in Congress under the slogan "This woman's place is in the House—the House of Representatives." She quickly became a champion for the environment and for society's underdogs, especially women and minorities.

Not everyone liked her style. Writer Norman Mailer said that Abzug's voice "could boil the fat off a taxicab driver's neck." And although President Jimmy Carter hired Abzug to head up a Women's Commission in 1977, he ended up firing her later. Abzug's husband, Martin, joked, "[Bella's] the only one I know who can get fired from a nonpaying job."

What was Abzug's main concern? That same year, she said, "Our struggle today is not to have a female Einstein get appointed as an assistant professor. It is for a woman schlemiel to get as quickly promoted as a male schlemiel."

MAKING A DIFFERENCE

In 1915, Alice Miller jokingly argued that men were unfit to vote because they were too emotional and violent. She wrote, "Their conduct at baseball games and at political conventions confirms this." Of course, Miller's idea cannot be carried out because the Constitution states that voters can't be discriminated against on the basis of race, sex, and age.

BUT (and this is a big "but") in the 2000 case of *Bush v. Gore,* the Supreme Court found that "the individual citizen has no federal constitutional right to vote . . . for the President of the United States"! That's because the Constitution doesn't actually *state* that all citizens have the right to vote—it just says that they can't be *discriminated* against!

Boy, that's tricky. Of the 119 nations that elect politicians to all levels of government, *eleven* don't provide the right to vote in their constitutions. The United States is one of them.

Clearly there must be some very clever reason for this. Please research the matter and then explain why this is so. While it may take years or even your entire lifetime to accomplish the task, I'm sure it will be worth it. (If it helps, I can mail you some energy bars.)

Brilliant Leaders

"THE IGNORANCE OF ONE VOTER IN A DEMOCRACY IMPAIRS THE SECURITY OF ALL." —*John F. Kennedy*

Who was the most brilliant United States president? To find out, the journal *Political Psychology* published a study comparing the IQ and "intellectual openness" of all United States presidents.

Since dead presidents do poorly on tests, *Political Psychology* based presidential performance on surveys by political scientists and presidential historians.

Intelligence was just one of more than two dozen traits the group analyzed. When the results were in, the group found that intelligence was the only trait that consistently tied in with "presidential greatness."

Since John Quincy Adams had the highest IQ results (his score was between 165–175), he gets the nod as the most intelligent American president. (Pretty good for someone whose grandmother couldn't read!) At the other end, Warren Harding scored the lowest of any president in the last 110 years.

★ *THE WHITE HOUSE HAS THIRTY-TWO BATHROOMS. DO YOU THINK WARREN HARDING COULD COUNT THAT HIGH?*

"Intellectual openness," or "seriously considering different points of view," was also tested in this same study. On a scale of 0–100, Bill Clinton and John F. Kennedy both scored 82, and Abraham Lincoln scored a 95. But coming in first place was Thomas Jefferson with an astounding 99.1! (George W. Bush scored a "0" in this category. It was the lowest score registered.)

No such study has been done of our vice presidents, even though they have all been just a heartbeat away from a promotion. All it takes is for the president to die. And this harsh fact led to one of the cruelest moments in vice presidential history:

In 1919, Vice President Thomas Marshall's speech in Atlanta was interrupted by word that President Woodrow Wilson had just died. An amazed Marshall told the crowd, "I must leave at once to take up my duties as Chief Executive." For the next hour, he got busy arranging to get back to Washington, D.C., where he would become . . . nothing! Marshall later got word that the president was actually quite alive. Tarnation! "A most cruel hoax," was how he later described the incident.

But hey, no matter what their IQ scores are, ALL presidents get paid. Currently the president makes $400,000 a year, and various expense accounts add another $70,000 in spending money. Upon retirement, former presidents get $300,000 for expenses, and former First Ladies (and Gentlemen) get $20,000 just for existing.

HIS HIGHNESS, THE PRESIDENT OF THE UNITED STATES, AND THE PROTECTOR OF ITS LIBERTIES

As the first president of the United States, George Washington made $25,000 a year. By some estimates, in today's money that would be almost exactly what the president makes now! But despite the big bucks, Washington wasn't thrilled about being president. He described his emotions upon taking office as being like "those of a culprit going to his place of execution."

Washington was handsome, built like

a linebacker, and born to a family with impressive land holdings.[1] But as a war hero with a wholesome image, Washington's incredible popularity annoyed his peers. John Adams wrote, "The . . . roaring of the word Washington, Washington, Washington . . . deafens, stuns, astonishes and bedizzards all who are within hearing." (Yes, "bedizzards"!) Adams grew so jealous of the man he once called a "muttonhead" that even when counting off Washington's good points, Adams couldn't help adding that "reading, thinking, or writing" were not among them. (Cold, John, very cold.)

Once Washington was president, he would not shake hands because he thought it was unpresidential. (He preferred a nice presidential bow.) While this might lead you to think that he was stuffy, to Washington's credit, he insisted upon being called "Mr. President," as opposed

---

1. Local Indians nicknamed Washington's great-grandfather "Town Taker" for his skill in parting them from their land.

to the title the Senate tried to push on him: "His Highness, the President of the United States, and the Protector of Its Liberties."

But never mind all that now. What you really want to know about is *money*. Take a close look at Washington's portrait on the one-dollar bill. His expression is a bit awkward, isn't it? (If it's not, mail the dollar to me, and I'll send you a better one.)

By the time he became president, Washington only had one tooth left in his head, and by the time his "dollar-bill" portrait was done, that holdout was long gone. That's why his mouth and jaw protrude a bit—he was wearing Revolutionary dentures.

Washington's dentures were not wooden; this myth may have come about because his dentist was named John Greenwood. Washington had four sets of dentures, and the nicest set was made with gold springs, hippo and elephant ivory, human teeth, and portions of horse and donkey teeth. (The ivory teeth turned black when Washington drank certain wines. *Yech*!)

Many dentures from colonial times were made from the teeth of young adults who met an early end. Dentists were known as ghoulish individuals who roamed battle-fields with a pair of pliers and a pouch. (Just like today!)

Now let's get back to the dollar. Yes, it would be nice to have a thousand of them, but never mind that. Washington's dollar-bill portrait was done in 1796 by a man named Gilbert Stuart. Stuart painted Washington many times, and it was usually a frustrating experience.[2] Since Washington had to endure many long sittings while being painted, he often withdrew into a Zen-like state for them. In short, Washington zoned out.

Stuart complained that "an apathy seemed to seize him, and a vacuity spread over his countenance." And so that's what we got for the dollar portrait: a vacuous Founding Father.

THE TASTE OF FREEDOM

Thomas Jefferson was arguably the most brilliant leader our nation has seen. His favorite book was Virgil's *Aeneid* (in its

---

2. *One of Stuart's most famous of these paintings was saved by Dolley Madison in 1814, when she fled the soon-to-be-burned White House.*

original Latin) AND he invented the dumbwaiter. But he liked the lottery so much, he thought *everyone* should play it. Go figure! Among his many contributions to politics and the arts, Jefferson can also be thanked for showing us that cheese is the food of religious freedom.

In 1802, the citizens of Cheshire, Massachusetts, sent an interesting "thank-you" gift to Jefferson at the White House. To show their appreciation of his spirited defense of religious freedom, the townspeople sent him a wheel of cheese weighing over half a ton.

A grateful Jefferson began eating the cheese on the spot. He was probably wearing his pajamas as he did so. (Jefferson even greeted ambassadors at the White House in his jammies.) This illustrates how many truly brilliant people can seem eccentric to the casual observer. For instance, Jefferson proposed that new states in the west be given names like Metropotamia, Pelisipia, and Polypotamia. I'm sure there were very good reasons to do this. (I have no idea what they could have been.)

THE ADAMS FAMILY

John Adams was one of our most brilliant presidents. But what a temper! Secretary of War James McHenry once called our second president "absolutely insane," but he probably exaggerated. Luckily for Adams, his wife, Abigail, was funny, literate, affectionate, and devoted to both her husband and her country. Abigail was certainly the first great First Lady, and she proved the perfect counterbalance for John.

The son of the nation's first power couple was John Quincy Adams. Though Abigail said she'd rather see her son "thrown as a log on the fire than see him president of the United States," that didn't stop him from serving in the White House from 1825 to 1829. Befitting his brilliant lineage, John Quincy Adams began his professional career at age fourteen, serving as a translator for American diplomats in Russia!

Herein is a problem with brilliant people. What if their children don't burn as brightly? John Quincy Adams was a self-described "cold, austere, and forbidding" man, who browbeat his three sons mercilessly for their "mediocrity." When he wrapped up his presidential term, he announced plans to move to Massachusetts where his oldest son, George

Washington Adams, lived. There, the statesman could devote his full attention to getting George on track. But the idea of unlimited father-son time was so unappealing to his son, George threw himself into the cold waters of Long Island Sound.

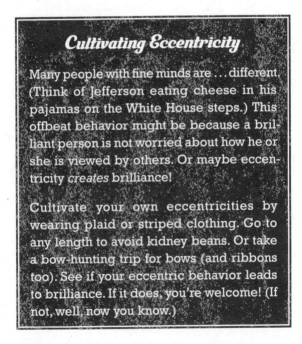

Cultivating Eccentricity

Many people with fine minds are ... different. (Think of Jefferson eating cheese in his pajamas on the White House steps.) This offbeat behavior might be because a brilliant person is not worried about how he or she is viewed by others. Or maybe eccentricity *creates* brilliance!

Cultivate your own eccentricities by wearing plaid or striped clothing. Go to any length to avoid kidney beans. Or take a bow-hunting trip for bows (and ribbons too). See if your eccentric behavior leads to brilliance. If it does, you're welcome! (If not, well, now you know.)

Setting tragedy aside, John Quincy Adams ran for and was elected to the House of Representatives. His greatness there is unquestioned; when Congress enacted a ban on the reading of abolitionist petitions in 1836, Adams began the next session by reading an abolitionist petition, and he *continued* doing so at each new session until the gag rule was struck down in 1844. Also to his great credit, he defended the Africans aboard the slave ship *Amistad*.

OUR BRILLIANT NUTMEG DEALER

Abraham Lincoln is an American legend. After all, he was the only president born in a log cabin that he built with his own hands. (Wait, darn it, my second-grade history notes can't be right!)

What IS true is that Lincoln was a man of almost superhuman powers of brilliance. And he wasn't just all brains, either. He was also the best wrestler of any president. Just before he entered politics, Lincoln once wrestled the leader of a local band of toughs and did so well, the rough-and-tumble gang members attended the rest of his local debates. And he once tossed a troublemaker at a political rally out a door and onto his butt.

But just as amazing, Lincoln had an incredible ability to keep his perspective and not take things personally. Making decisions about controversial topics like slavery and states' rights guaranteed Lincoln's unpopularity with certain groups of people. And so Abe was subjected to the worst abuse imaginable. Lincoln was called "The Baboon" so often, it became his nickname. One South Carolina newspaper even called him a "horrid-looking wretch . . . sooty and scoundrelly . . . a cross between the nutmeg dealer [and] the horse swapper."[3]

---

3. Harper's Weekly *simply made a list describing Abe: "Filthy Story-Teller, Despot, Liar, Thief, Braggart, Buffoon, Usurper, Monster, Ignoramus Abe, Old Scoundrel, Perjurer, Robber, Swindler, Tyrant, Field-Butcher, Land-Pirate."*

Can you believe the nerve? They compared Lincoln to a nutmeg dealer! Of course, better this than a sharp stick in the eye . . . or a bullet in the back of the head.

You should already know a fair amount about Lincoln's assassination, so let me just add that the White House was open to the public in the eighteenth and nineteenth centuries. In the confusion following Lincoln's death, scores of unscrupulous scumbags simply walked into the White House, grabbed a souvenir or three, and walked out. Among other things, more than $20,000 of White House china was lost this way after Abe's death.

Lincoln's subordinates were often incompetent, and their stupidity was on full display during the attempts to bury the president. In an amazing exhibition of government botchery, after Lincoln's initial funeral and burial in Springfield, Illinois, he was subsequently dug up twelve times from that very same graveyard!

The Worst of the Firsts (and Her Firstborn)

Abraham Lincoln kept the country together, but after his death, his own family fell apart in a most uncivil war. This was partially due to the fact that brilliant people don't always marry sensibly. Lincoln's wife, Mary Todd Lincoln, was a proud woman, but not so proud that she minded people seeing her chasing Abe through town while swinging a knife.

Why was she the worst First Lady in history? Well, she may have been insane. Or perhaps Mrs. Lincoln just didn't appreciate Abe's sense of humor. At six feet four inches tall, Lincoln would introduce himself and Mary (who was five feet two inches tall) to people as "the long and the short of the presidency." That was still better than her nickname: the She-Wolf.

People with difficult personalities sometimes mellow with age. Not Mary. After Abe's assassination, it took her five weeks to move out of the White House, which was a bit of a drag for incoming president Andrew Johnson. Mary's erratic behavior and outrageous spending habits were especially galling for her firstborn son, Robert. Robert had his mother officially charged with lunacy in a court of law.

Mary was eventually released back into society, whereupon the long and bitter struggle between she and Robert continued. Calling her son a "monster of mankind," she severed all relations with him.

The initial reasons for his disinterment/ reinterment had to do with getting Abe laid to rest in his very own monument. But after a foiled 1876 attempt to kidnap (or corpse-nap) Abe's body, he was reburied in a vault under the tomb.

In 1901, Abe's son, Robert, ordered his father buried beneath thick concrete. But before this final final burial, workers double-checked to make sure Abe was still in his coffin. He was. As the coffin lid came off, the gathered spectators could see that Abe's beard and mole were still there. But while the great man had been embalmed into a preserved union, the American flag on his chest had vaporized.

ANARCHY SUCKS

William McKinley was the first president to make campaign phone calls. Running against him was William Jennings Bryan, a man noted for his long speeches. To mock this, McKinley's team handed out minia-ture coffins to voters. The coffins had the words "Talked to Death" on them.

President McKinley is usually remem-bered for being assassinated in 1901. This was a shame, because McKinley was a brilliant president. He was perhaps the first notable United States leader to

> ### *Bon Voyage, Grand Mal*
>
> McKinley was extremely devoted to his wife, Ida, who suffered from epileptic seizures. Yet after her husband's assassination, Ida's seizures disappeared.

effectively oppose big business interests and monopolies. While his first term was marked by land-grabbing (he snagged Hawaii, Guam, Puerto Rico, and, to a lesser extent, the Philippines and Cuba), his second term began with his arguing in favor of reciprocal trade agreements with foreign countries.

The day after he announced this new policy, an anarchist named Leon Czolgosz shot him dead. Thanks for nothing, punk!

THE SUPERMAN

Even if Teddy Roosevelt (president from 1901–09) had never become president, he still would have been famous. He climbed the Matterhorn, was multilingual, wrote dozens of books, and boxed with heavy-weight champion John Sullivan in a bout that left Teddy blind in one eye. He was such a loveable character, Mark Twain called him "the most popular human being that has ever existed in the United States."

Once Roosevelt took over for the assassi-nated McKinley, he went about destroying

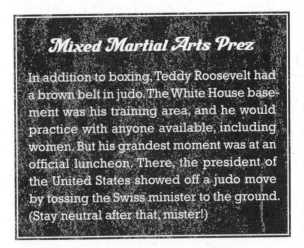

Mixed Martial Arts Prez

In addition to boxing, Teddy Roosevelt had a brown belt in judo. The White House base-ment was his training area, and he would practice with anyone available, including women. But his grandest moment was at an official luncheon. There, the president of the United States showed off a judo move by tossing the Swiss minister to the ground. (Stay neutral after that, mister!)

monopolies and fighting big business. Just as impressive, Roosevelt was an ardent environmentalist who set aside huge areas of land for conservation and parks.

Roosevelt was a man of contrasts:

★ HE WAS A WARMONGER WHO WON THE NOBEL PEACE PRIZE.

★ HE WAS A FIERY PUBLIC SPEAKER WHOSE MOTTO WAS "SPEAK SOFTLY BUT CARRY A BIG STICK."

★ ALTHOUGH HE (OR HIS STAFF MEMBERS) MAY HAVE ACCEPTED ILLEGAL CAMPAIGN CONTRIBUTIONS, A DISGUSTED MILLIONAIRE COMPLAINED, "WE BOUGHT THE SON OF A B**** AND THEN HE DID NOT STAY BOUGHT."

★ WHILE HE DIDN'T ALWAYS TAKE CARE OF THE UNDERDOG, ONE OF ROOSEVELT'S FIRST ACTS AS PRESIDENT WAS TO HAVE BOOKER T. WASHINGTON OVER TO THE WHITE HOUSE.

In addition to having the coolest dying words of all time ("Please put out the light"), Teddy should be remembered for an achievement so profound, it has stuck in my mind ever since I learned about it five minutes ago:

He had an aide named Archie Butt.

HE FELT THE EARTH MOVE UNDER HIS FEET

Yes, President William Taft (in office from 1909–13) was overweight, and he knew it. He even took some pleasure in repeating a telegram exchange he had with the Secretary of War, Elihu Root.

Giving "Gravitas" New Meaning

Taft was so oversized, he once got stuck in the White House bathtub. And he had a valet on hand to tie his shoes for him.

Taft cabled, "Took long horseback today; feeling fine."

Root's response: "How is the horse?"

The fact that Taft found humor in this story is an encouraging sign of his brilliance. Another signifier of his oversized intellect was his interest in the law. After serving as president, he went on to become the Chief Justice of the United States Supreme Court for the last nine years of his life.

Taft was also a real athlete. After all, he was the first president who played golf. (This should tell you something about golf.) And he was also the first president to begin a baseball season by throwing out the pitch to start the game. (Hmmm, this tells you nothing at all. That makes it perfect for this book!)

But not everything about Taft was huge. When Teddy Roosevelt ran against him for the Republican presidential nomination, he said that Taft had "brains less than a guinea pig." Though Roosevelt hand-picked Taft as his successor, he felt big Bill hadn't worked hard enough at conserving natural resources and breaking up big business trusts. The old joke that "Taft" stood for "Take Advice From Teddy" no longer applied.

Not So Brilliant I

Warren Gamaliel (!) Harding is thought to be the worst president of the twentieth century. Journalist H. L. Mencken wrote, "No other such complete and dreadful nitwit is to be found in the pages of American history."

SILENCE SPEAKS VOLUMES . . . (I THINK)

"When a great many people are unable to find work, unemployment results." *Ha!* President Calvin Coolidge (in office from 1923–29) said that. Why is Coolidge one of my favorite presidents? Is it because he liked to ring the White House doorbell and run off before the servants could answer it? Maybe! Or was it because he said, "The American people want a solemn ass as president, and I think I'll go along with them"? Perhaps! Or maybe it's because he had an electric horse installed at the White House so he could ride it!

Calvin "Silent Cal" Coolidge didn't like to talk much. In fact, there are many famous stories about what he *didn't* say. At his press conferences, Coolidge would not allow himself to be quoted. He often made reporters write their questions down, and then he would go through the pile and answer only the ones he wanted to.

Once in a while, Coolidge went through the pile and didn't find any questions he liked. "I have no questions today," he'd say, and then he would walk out without cracking a smile. But you just know he had to be laughing on the inside.[4]

---

4. *At one press conference, Coolidge answered "No" to all the questions. Then, as the reporters left, he shouted after them that he was still off the record!*

Coolidge's wife, Grace, was much more outgoing than her husband. Shortly after their marriage, Coolidge handed Grace a bag full of holey socks. Grace asked, "Did you marry me to darn your socks?"

Coolidge's deadpan response: "No, but I find it mighty handy."

★ CALVIN COOLIDGE IS THE ONLY PRESIDENT TO BE BORN ON THE FOURTH OF JULY.

A presidential biographer wrote that Coolidge and Grace once visited a chicken farm where Grace saw a rooster having sex with a hen. The embarrassed farmer told her that the rooster engaged in the act many times each day.

Grace smiled and requested that the farmer tell that to her husband.

After the farmer did so, Coolidge asked, "To the same hen?" When the farmer said, "No," Coolidge instructed him, "Tell that to Mrs. Coolidge."

But the most famous story about this tight-lipped president is probably the one where a woman at a party came up to the president.

"My husband has bet me that I won't get more than two words out of you all night!" she said teasingly.

"You lose," said Coolidge.

FDR AND MAD MAGAZINE

Now we get to a record-breakingly brilliant leader. Not only was Franklin Delano Roosevelt the only four-term president, but he is also the only president to hold an athletic record that still stands. As a high school student, FDR set a record for the standing high jump. (This event is pretty much what it sounds like.) Since the event was retired from competition, FDR still holds the record today.

This athletic feat is even more unusual as FDR was also the only paraplegic American president. While it's no secret *now* that FDR was paralyzed by adult-onset polio, it is remarkable how well his secret was kept during his life. There are only two photographs of FDR in his wheelchair, and it wasn't until 2001 that a statue of him in a wheelchair was added to his memorial in Washington, D.C.

Born to a rich family, it was a bit odd that Franklin Delano Roosevelt would be

It's Time to Act Out!

Civil War reenactors dress up in costume and "act out" historic battles from yesteryear. But you never hear about World War II reenactments—until now!

Study crucial battles from World War II and then arm your forces with water guns, rubber bands (remember eye protection!), or paintball guns. The winning side can sing a historically accurate song from the era, such as "We Are the Champions (of a Democratic Republic Once Formerly the Colony of an Overseas Power)."

president during the Great Depression. He endorsed the "New Deal" as a way to reinvigorate the economy, but not everyone was a fan of it. One-time New Deal supporter Hugh Johnson called it the work of "a cockeyed crew of wand-waving wizards."

We can thank people like Johnson for inspiring *Mad* magazine's future mascot, the cock-eyed kid later named Alfred E. Newman. Roosevelt-haters invented his foolishly grinning face to show how stupid a typical FDR supporter was.

FDR's wife, Eleanor, was also born a Roosevelt. In fact, the two were fifth cousins once removed. (Please don't ask me to explain.) "It's a good thing to keep the name in the family," said Eleanor's uncle, Teddy Roosevelt.

Eleanor started off in life as a timid orphan, but she eventually developed into a confident politico. She was the first First Lady to hold her own press conferences, and also the first to carry a gun. And Eleanor must have been tempted to pop a cap in her mother-in-law, Sara Roosevelt.

Sara was a fairly terrible woman, telling Eleanor's children that she herself was their "real mother," and undermining Eleanor at every turn. Sara even lived in an adjoining townhome to Franklin and Eleanor. Sara remodeled the homes so that she could walk through a door on any floor of her son's home that she pleased.

Regarding her mother-in-law's death in 1940, Eleanor wrote, "It is dreadful to have lived so close to someone for thirty-six years and feel no deep affection or sense of loss."

Eleanor's cousin (and Teddy Roosevelt's daughter), Alice, was also a vile creature. She often made fun of Eleanor's protruding teeth and called her friends "female impersonators." The year that FDR was running for a third term against Wendell Willkie, Alice was asked if she'd vote for FDR. "I'd rather vote for Hitler," was her response.

It was during that campaign that Eleanor knew she had arrived on the national scene. Willkie's presidential campaign ran slogans like "We Don't Want Eleanor Either."

TO ERR IS TRUMAN

You have to like Harry S Truman (in office from 1945–53). It takes guts and a wicked sense of humor to order the pilot of the presidential airplane (called the *Sacred Cow*) to buzz the White House. That's what Truman did on a day when his wife, Bess, and daughter were enjoying some fun on the White House roof. (The stunt succeeded in giving a thrill to pretty much everyone in Washington, D.C.)

Even though Truman's education was limited to a high school diploma, he had a great way with words. When Truman fired the popular General Douglas

Washington's Dirty Laundry

Bess Truman didn't find Washington, D.C., laundries up to snuff, so she mailed all of her dirty clothes back to her home state of Missouri.

Not So Brilliant II

Harry Truman made a brilliant insight when he said Richard Nixon was "a shifty, g****** liar, and people know it." While Nixon did accomplish good things (three cheers for the Environmental Protection Agency!), he resigned from the presidency in disgrace for repeatedly lying. By saying, "I am not a crook," he even managed to lie about being a liar.

MacArthur, he said, "I didn't fire him because he was a dumb son-of-a-b****, although he was, but that's not against the law for generals. If it was, half to three-quarters of them would be in jail."

And back when he was told that FDR

wanted him as a vice president, the surprised Truman said, "Tell him to go to hell." I guess he really earned his nickname. (No, not "Sassy Pants," though that was one of them. He was also known as "Give 'Em Hell Harry.")

PRESIDENTIAL PASTRY

John F. Kennedy (in office from 1960–63) is the most written-about president in modern history. Sadly, he wasn't around long enough for us to judge him by his achievements. But Kennedy sure had the potential to be a brilliant president. Particularly noteworthy: the creation of the Peace Corps, his focus on NASA and the moon program, and his ability to inspire the "best and the brightest" to go into government service.

Kennedy was a gifted writer, winning a Pulitzer Prize for his book *Profiles in Courage*. He could speak good too. On June 26, 1963, he gave his famous speech at the Berlin Wall. It included the line, "Today, in the world of freedom the proudest boast is 'Ich bin ein Berliner.'" This was intended to translate to "I am a Berliner" (that is, a native of Berlin), but the word *Berliner* can also mean a "jelly doughnut." (Berliners can be found all over Germany; they have sugar on top and strawberry jelly inside.)

But Kennedy's *context* was clear. He really wasn't trying to say, "I am a jelly doughnut." That would have been kooky!

★ *KENNEDY MEANS "UGLY HEAD" IN GAELIC.*

Life's a Gas

Gerald Ford followed Richard Nixon into the White House, and he proved to be a likable leader despite one bad trait: he had the worst gas of any United States president. He was notorious among his Secret Service bodyguards for letting one rip, and then looking around in surprised dismay and saying, "C'mon, show a little class!"

As for the Pulitzer Prize Kennedy won for his book *Profiles in Courage,* debates over its authorship puts the book in the same category as Kennedy's presidency: "The brilliance that might have been."

WHAT, BEHIND THE RABBIT?

As a youth, Jimmy Carter was a very bright young man who studied nuclear physics in the Navy. Even so, nobody thought he'd become leader of the nation. Carter didn't exude the seriousness of a world leader. I mean, he reported seeing a UFO in 1969!

When Carter announced he was running for president, his own mother asked, "President of what?" Once he was in the White House (1976–1980), he came up with a new policy called a national "Energy Plan." It ran out of gas after his presidency, but he gets points for trying.

Two things doomed Carter's reelection hopes. One was the kidnapping of a number of American hostages in Iran. Carter referred to the botched military operation to save them as an "incomplete success." (I guess the same words could apply to any president's administration!)[5]

The other thing was a killer rabbit.

---

5. *As an ex-president, Carter put to shame the other former chief executives out playing golf while he built Habitats for Humanity and brokered Mideast peace deals.*

Carter was fishing in a pond on his farm when he spotted something swimming toward him. It was a gigantic swamp rabbit. If you think that sounds cute, think again. This rabbit was apparently berserk. It was making hissing sounds and swimming toward the presidential

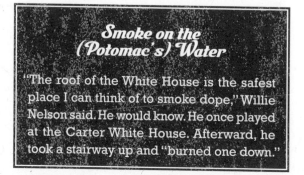

Smoke on the (Potomac's) Water

"The roof of the White House is the safest place I can think of to smoke dope," Willie Nelson said. He would know. He once played at the Carter White House. Afterward, he took a stairway up and "burned one down."

canoe, intent on boarding it!

Carter did the smart thing: he drove the enraged beast off with his paddle. But when the press got wind of the story, it was front-page news the next day. Somehow, the news of the president being attacked by a killer rabbit was so silly, it gave him an image problem.

IF YOU AIN'T DUTCH, YOU AIN'T MUCH

The popular president Ronald "Dutch" Reagan is often remembered for his fierce opposition to communism. But Reagan wasn't always so dead-set against the

207

commies. According to presidential biographer Edmund Morris, Reagan was a longtime Democrat who was denied admission to the Communist Party in 1938. He was rebuffed because it was

It's a Record!

More appointees of Ronald Reagan were implicated, accused, or indicted in criminal activity than any other United States president. (Second place: Warren Harding.)

feared he was not sufficiently dedicated to the cause!

So Reagan remained a Democrat until the 1960s, when he switched parties. His conversion set up one of the great upsets in United States debate history. In 1967, Ronald Reagan debated the formidable Robert F. Kennedy. According to *Newsweek,* "Political rookie Reagan . . . left old campaigner Kennedy blinking when the session ended." Kennedy conceded defeat and Reagan was on the national map.

Part of Ronald's popularity came from his squeaky-clean image. Even in the diary he kept as president, he avoided swear words, writing "h___l" and "d___" instead. But he did have a tendency to stretch the truth if it helped make a good story. He even told Israel's prime minister that he filmed the liberation of Nazi concentration camps as a United States soldier during WWII.

That was a good one, since he never

served in Europe at all! Reagan's love of a good story meant he liked to tell long jokes. One of his favorites was about a charity volunteer who phoned a wealthy man named Mr. Jones.

"MR. JONES," THE VOLUNTEER SAID, "OUR RECORDS SHOW THAT YOU HAVE NEVER GIVEN US A CENT."

"AND DO YOUR RECORDS SHOW I HAVE AN ELDERLY MOTHER WITH NO MONEY?" MR. JONES ANSWERED.

"WELL, NO," THE VOLUNTEER ADMITTED.

"DO THEY SHOW I HAVE A CRIPPLED BROTHER OR A WIDOWED SISTER WITH FIVE CHILDREN?"

"NO."

"WELL," MR. JONES CONCLUDED, "IF I DON'T DO ANYTHING FOR THEM, WHY WOULD I DO ANYTHING FOR YOU?"

Shining with a Lesser Light

One controversial aspect of the presidency of George W. Bush had to do with torture. Not the torture of suspected terrorists, but the torture the American public had to endure when he gave speeches! Here are some examples of his maltreatment of innocent words:

"One of the great things about books is, sometimes there are some fantastic pictures."

"I know how hard it is to put food on your family."

"I understand small business growth. I was one."

"I know that the human being and the fish can coexist peacefully."

"As I'm sure you can imagine, it is an unimaginable honor to live here."

"I want everybody to hear loud and clear that I'm going to be the president of everybody."

"There's an old saying . . . that says, fool me once, shame on—shame on you. Fool me—you can't get fooled again."[7]

7. The saying is "Fool me once, shame on you. Fool me twice, shame on me." There is also a Klingon version: "Fool me once, shame on you. Fool me twice, prepare to die."

POETRY PROMPT!

President George W. Bush once said, "I don't make verbal gaffes. I'm speaking in the perfect forms and rhythms of ancient haiku." Following the president's examples, practice combining words and phrases in a creative way. You'll be amazed at how easy it can be to express yourself like a somewhat befuddled poet.

AT THE DINNER TABLE: "You have no disregard for gravy!"

ARRIVING AT SOMEONE ELSE'S HOUSE: "I come to here today as a human being and a sportsman."

TAKING OFF YOUR COAT: "Removing this jacket was the right decision yesterday, it is the right decision now, and it will be the right decision ever."

INSPIRING OTHERS: "So long as I'm alive, my measure of success will be victory—and success."

THE JURY IS OUT

The average IQ for a college graduate in the United States is about 115. Barack Obama graduated *magna cum laude* from Harvard Law School, where he served as editor of the *Harvard Law Review.* He also taught for years at the University of Chicago. But just as promising, he explained how he got into politics this way: *"I did what I often do when I'm confronted with a difficult decision. I prayed on it. Amen. And then I asked my wife. Amen. And, after consulting these two higher powers . . ."*

Great Expectorations

"READER, SUPPOSE YOU WERE AN IDIOT; AND SUPPOSE YOU WERE A MEMBER OF CONGRESS; BUT I REPEAT MYSELF." —*Mark Twain*

Boy, Mark Twain didn't think the average politician in Congress was very bright. But maybe he just needed to meet Congressman John Dingell of Michigan. Dingell has been in office since 1955. He's served *twenty-seven consecutive terms*![1]

---

1. *Members of the House of Representatives serve two-year terms. (Note to John: How about giving someone else a chance?)*

With that kind of genius for reelection, the man must be a member of Mensa.

★ *MENSA MEMBERS HAVE TO SHOW THAT THEIR IQ RANKS IN THE TOP 2 PERCENT OF THE POPULATION. ONE OF THEIR PRIMARY GOALS IS TO INCREASE HUMAN INTELLIGENCE FOR THE BENEFIT OF HUMANITY. BRILLIANT!*

If *your* Mensa group met at the White House, you'd only have to walk about a mile down Pennsylvania Avenue to get to John Dingell's office on Capitol Hill. That's where the two houses of Congress meet to make and pass laws. Congress is officially made up of the House of Representatives (435 mostly brilliant members) and the Senate (100 generally brilliant members).

How do I know these politicians are brilliant? For one thing, they've given themselves a staff of 102 "pages." Pages are teenagers in charge of running errands. So a senator needing to deliver a document just pages a page to pick up a page. Congressional pages are always high-achieving high school juniors, currently paid about $20,000 a year for

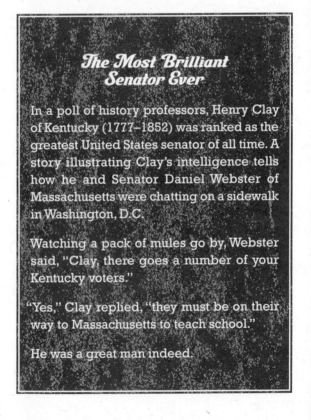

The Most Brilliant Senator Ever

In a poll of history professors, Henry Clay of Kentucky (1777–1852) was ranked as the greatest United States senator of all time. A story illustrating Clay's intelligence tells how he and Senator Daniel Webster of Massachusetts were chatting on a sidewalk in Washington, D.C.

Watching a pack of mules go by, Webster said, "Clay, there goes a number of your Kentucky voters."

"Yes," Clay replied, "they must be on their way to Massachusetts to teach school."

He was a great man indeed.

one semester's work.[2] They are usually among the smartest high school students in the United States.

If that's not brilliant, I don't know what is!

But as smart as pages are, the savviest people in Washington, D.C., are *lobbyists*. These are private citizens and groups who try to influence the decisions of the members of Congress. How do lobbyists do this? They cajole, threaten, and sometimes even use bribes. But can these very well-paid people actually make a difference in United States policies? Well, let's just say that lobbyists aren't known as the unofficial "Third House of Congress" for nothing.

Lobbyists multiply like rabbits, if you can imagine rabbits that cajole, threaten, and bribe. In 2000, there were about 17,000

2. *If a page's parent was also a page, the politicians say, "You're a page out of the old book." This is considered funny.*

217

I Guess He Wasn't Fund-raising

In the 1930s, Congressman John McGroarty wrote this letter to a constituent: "One of the countless drawbacks of being in Congress is that I . . . receive impertinent letters from a jackass like you. . . . Will you please take two running jumps and go to hell."

lobbyists in Washington, D.C. By 2008, there were 34,000 of them. They *doubled!* At this rate, there will be more than 130,000 lobbyists in the United States capital by 2024. The poor senators and representatives don't stand a chance unless they develop some means of defense.

Luckily, I have a solution: spit! Taking inspiration from their colleagues of yesteryear, today's politicians can use their salivary glands to drive lobbyists away. And why not? There have been spitting images on Capitol Hill from Day One. For instance, in 1798, Representative

Matthew Lyon of Vermont walked across the House floor and hawked a loogie in the face of someone who was annoying him. (Lyon's victim later nailed him in the head with a hickory stick as payback.)

In 1837, a newspaper report described how congressional pages slipped on the "disgusting compound of tobacco juice, wafers and sand" that covered the House of Representatives' floor. (Maybe *that's* why Oscar Wilde said, "America is one long expectoration.") And when novelist Charles Dickens visited Capitol Hill, he was shocked at how the politicians propped their feet up on desks while they spat tobacco juice all over the place. Sure, there were cuspidors (aka spittoons), but you were as likely to miss your shot as to hit it.

★ *CHARLES DICKENS ALSO HEARD ONE CONGRESSMAN THREATEN TO CUT THE THROAT OF ANOTHER. TO THE WRITER'S AMAZEMENT, NOBODY THOUGHT MUCH OF IT, AND BUSINESS CONTINUED AS USUAL: ACH-TOOIE!*

GOOD NEWS AND BAD NEWS

Imagine coming to Washington, D.C., in 1800, the year it was established as the nation's capital. And also pretend that you're a newly elected representative. Hurray for you! The people have spoken, and they say you're all right.[3] But the same can't be said for the capital. There are vacant lots everywhere, the streets are muddy, it's ferociously hot and humid, and pigs roam the streets.

In short: this place sucks!

No worries. You're smart, and you know that the nation's capital has been moved twice already. Therefore, you try enacting legislation to get it moved again, this time to someplace a little more agreeable, like Buffalo or San Diego. But when debate on moving the capital a third time hits

---

3. *From 1787 to 1913, United States senators were appointed by their state legislature. So senators tended to be more truly political than the salt-of-the-earth representatives.*

the Senate floor, Washington, D.C., residents show up in the gallery to protest the move. The protesters make such a stink that Senator James Jackson of Georgia suggests the military shoot the lot of them. (And he isn't kidding.)

If you'd actually been there, you could have told Senator Jackson that he didn't need the military. The politicians could

Special Olympics

Senator Strom Thurmond holds the record for the longest filibuster by a single senator. In 1957, he went on a twenty-four-hour-and-eighteen-minute filibuster to stop a civil rights bill. Leading up to the filibuster, he took steam baths and dehydrated himself so that he wouldn't need to use the restroom.

Senators can team up for a filibuster, like the eighty-three-day filibuster southern senators ran to unsuccessfully block passage of the 1964 Civil Rights Act.

221

have done their own shooting! In the 1800s, pretty much everyone carried guns into government buildings. I'm talking about politicians, judges, and even visitors. Yep, visiting Congress was like visiting the Wild West.

Did government employees come to work heavily armed because they worried about violent anarchists, crazed abolitionists, and optimistic idealists?

Nope, it was their crazed *colleagues* who were dangerous. In 1832, Congressman William Stanbery pulled out his pistol and shot at Sam Houston, but his gun misfired. Eighteen years later, two quarreling senators drew pistols on each other, and one day in the House, a representative actually fired his gun on accident. Witnesses reported dozens of politicians drew iron and began waving their

Have Gun, Will Travel

If you visit the Capitol Building, go down the marble steps to the restaurant in the basement. There you will see the bloodstains of former representative William Taulbee. A reporter had written a story about Taulbee's numerous love affairs, thus ending his political career. Bad blood between the two worsened after Taulbee attacked the reporter and threatened his life. A chance meeting between the two on the stairway in 1890 led to Taulbee being shot to death. Since he acted in self-defense, the reporter was set free. (His having a gun in the seat of Congress was no big deal.)

Education in a Bottle

During Prohibition, a special room jokingly called the "Bureau of Education," magically opened in the Capitol Building. This was the spot where politicians of both parties could gather to play cards, drink alcohol, and smoke big cigars.

revolvers around. One senator observed that the only members of the House and Senate not armed with *one* gun were those who had "*two* revolvers and a Bowie knife." Even though Vice President Martin Van Buren carried two pistols when he presided at the Senate, that wouldn't have been enough to outgun Senator Ben Wade of Ohio, who liked to bring a sawed-off shotgun with him to the floor.

UNBRILLIANT LOWLIGHTS

Democrats and Republicans can work together, and sometimes even form *friendships* by treating each other with respect. Astounding! Of course, tempers can flare on Capitol Hill, making compromise impossible and resulting in unpleasant scenes.

1840: BATTLING CONGRESSMEN WILL MONTGOMERY AND KEN RAYNER BREAK THEIR CANES OVER EACH OTHER'S HEADS.

1860: AN ARGUMENT BETWEEN JOHN POTTER AND WILLIAM BARKSDALE TURNS INTO A WRESTLING MATCH ON THE FLOOR OF THE HOUSE. IN THE COURSE OF THE TUSSLE, POTTER TEARS OFF BARKSDALE'S WIG.

"I'VE SCALPED HIM!" POTTER CRIES, AND EVERYONE CHUCKLES. (SCALPING HUMOR WAS VERY POPULAR IN THE 1800S.)

1985: REPRESENTATIVE JIM WRIGHT OF TEXAS IS PRESIDING OVER THE HOUSE WHEN HE GRABS ANOTHER CONGRESSMAN BY THE ARM AND THREATENS TO KNOCK HIS TEETH OUT. IT'S A GOOD THING WRIGHT DOESN'T.

Consult Your Local Animal Doctor

Champ Clark was the Speaker of the House in the early 1900s, and so he acted as an umpire among the representatives. Clark was startled when a congressman's speech was interrupted by an Illinois representative who called out, "You're a jackass!"

After Clark told the name-caller to follow the rules of conduct, the representative said, "While I withdraw the unfortunate word, Mr. Speaker, I must insist the gentleman is out of order."

"How am I out of order?" asked the congressman who'd been called a jackass.

"Probably a veterinarian could tell you," said the other.

THE OTHER CONGRESSMAN—DAN LUNGREN—IS A MARTIAL ARTS EXPERT.

1995: AN EVENT NOW KNOWN AS THE "BRAWL IN THE HALL" TAKES PLACE IN FRONT OF TV CAMERAS AT THE HOUSE. POLITICIANS YELL AT EACH OTHER, AND DEMOCRAT SAM GIBBON OF FLORIDA GRABS AND PULLS THE NECKTIE OF REPUBLICAN BILL THOMAS. (THOMAS LATER GOT REVENGE BY TURNING OFF THE MICROPHONES AT A DEMOCRAT GATHERING. NICE!)

CRITICAL THINKING

Lobbyists are especially talented at giving their groups misleading names to hide their true intent. This allows them to be in favor of almost *anything* with nobody else being the wiser *(see following page)*:

LOBBY	PLATFORM
American Council on Science and Health	Argued that there's no link between fatty diets and heart disease
Committee for Energy Awareness	Funded by power utilities
Motherhood and Apple Pie Institute	A name that writer Howard Kurtz suggested for a lobby that could get away with anything
Washington Forest Protection Association	Favored abolishing logging restrictions
Clean Air Working Group	Worked to weaken the Clean Air Act
USA Foundation	Led by Jack Abramoff, who was convicted of fraud, tax evasion, and conspiracy to bribe public officials

Not-So-Brilliant *Villains*

"NOW YOU SEE THAT EVIL WILL ALWAYS TRIUMPH, BECAUSE GOOD IS DUMB." —Lord Dark Helmet

It's sad but true: in the course of history, untold millions have given in to greed and stupidity. This has led to unfortunate behaviors like cheating on pop quizzes and spying for other nations. Not only do these hare-brained villainous schemes hurt everyone, but when these villains get caught, their excuses are often really dopey.

This chapter is dedicated to some of the least brilliant villains ever. Let's start with the political leaders who forgot that they are supposed to be good role models!

HIT ME WITH YOUR BEST SHOT!

As immature as it sounds, leading politicians once regularly challenged each other to duels. While the idea of dueling was an imported tradition, even the Pilgrims dueled. (You'd be surprised at the damage big belt buckles can do.)

Once challenged to a duel, most men believed there was only one honorable way out. To fight! After all, any man refusing a duel could be called a "chicken," and the fact that he'd chickened out usually got printed up in the newspaper.

A BRILLIANT FEW THOUGHT OF CREATIVE WAYS TO GET OUT OF THEIR DUELS. FOR INSTANCE, GEORGIA POLITICIAN BENJAMIN HILL (1823–1882) SENT THIS MESSAGE TO HIS CHALLENGER IN ORDER TO BACK

OUT OF A DUEL: "I HAVE A SOUL TO SAVE AND A FAMILY TO SUPPORT AND YOU HAVE NEITHER." NICE ONE!

Washington, D.C., had a popular dueling spot called the "Dark and Bloody Grounds," which was the site of one of the most ludicrous duels ever. In 1836, Congressman Jesse Bynum of North Carolina and Daniel Jenifer of Maryland dueled there. Each man was armed with a pistol containing six shots. Standing at a distance of ten feet, the two started shooting at each other. After four shots, a

A Brilliant Idea!

In Japan, disgraced public figures have sometimes committed suicide to avoid the shame they have brought on their families. Maybe we could save lives by working out an exchange program with the Japanese: they ship their disgraced officials to us, and we send them ours.

witness asked when the duel would actually start.

Informed that the two men were already trying to kill each other, the witness exclaimed, "I thought they were jes' practicin'!" (Given their marksmanship, practicing would have been a good idea.)

The most infamous American duelist is Aaron Burr. One of just two vice presidents to shoot someone while in office, Burr was the only one to do so on purpose.[1] As Thomas Jefferson's vice president, Burr shot and killed famed Founding Father Alexander Hamilton.

Of course, Hamilton really asked for it. He once called Burr an "embryo-Caesar." I don't know about you, but them's fightin' words where I come from!

---

1. *The other was Dick Cheney. In 2006, during a hunting trip, he accidentally blasted a fellow hunter in the face with a shotgun.*

LUCKY NUMBER 13

James Wilkinson (1757–1825) was as slimy as they come. He was a double agent for the Spanish government *and* he double-crossed the traitor he was conspiring with! (If you double-cross a double-crosser, are you a quaduple-crosser?) Yep, Wilkinson was so despicably treacherous, he manages to make a murderer like Aaron Burr look good.

Oily from an early age, the money-hungry Wilkinson was gifted at ingratiating himself with important people. After the Revolutionary War, he moved to Kentucky, where he began his career as the double agent known as *Numero Trece* (number 13).

In 1787, Wilkinson secretly contacted agents of the Spanish government. He convinced the Spanish that if the price was right, he could get Kentucky declared as part of Spanish Louisiana. To show his "sincerity," he even took an oath of allegiance to the Spanish monarchy. Shortly afterward, he was promoted to general in the United States Army, and he duly reported on United States troop movements to the Spanish.

After Wilkinson's plot fell through, he hooked up with Aaron Burr and introduced Burr to his Spanish contacts. Burr had a dream of separating Louisiana from the United States and then invading Mexico. In this new plot, Burr was in charge of creating an army that the two men would persuade Britain to sponsor.

But no British money ever came in. As rumors of his involvement with Burr's scheme emerged, Wilkinson ratted Burr out to President Thomas Jefferson in 1806. Not knowing Wilkinson's role, the president ordered him to place Burr and his followers (known as "Burrites") under arrest!

Burr was captured and tried. As for Agent

13, Wilkinson survived a court martial and went on to lead United States forces in the War of 1812 so poorly, he was relieved of command. Disgraced after several congressional investigations, his good luck had finally run out. Wilkinson moved to Mexico, where he stayed until the end of his not-so *buenos días*.

THE POTTERIZER!

North Carolina state representative Robert Potter (1800–1842) once called an opponent "a squinting, skipping, squatting, squalling elf." So I guess you could say that Potter had an anger problem. (Plus, he didn't like elves.) While in office, Potter once attacked two

235

Raining Down Blows

In 1849, Missouri politician Francis Blair spied a rival on the sidewalk and attacked him with his umbrella. Blair was arrested and sentenced to one minute behind bars.

men (his own cousin and a preacher) and castrated both of them. (You don't want to know any more details.) He was convicted of, uh, you know, and spent six months in jail. Even so, it wasn't until he was caught cheating at cards that he was expelled from office!

Because of Potter's actions, North Carolina passed a law regarding "Malicious and Unlawful Maiming and Wounding," which made castration a hanging offense. Potter was later assassinated in Texas, but his name still lives on today: in some areas of the South, to "potterize" means to castrate.

THE LONG AND THE SHORT OF IT

In 1935, Louisiana senator Huey Long gave a fifteen-and-a-half-hour-long speech to block the passage of a bill he opposed. But even a notorious talker like Long must have run short of material for a speech of that length. How did he do it? Among other things, he simply read aloud from Shakespeare, fried-oyster recipes, and the Constitution. In the end, he had to go to the bathroom, and then the bill passed quicker than a kidney stone.

Point, Counterpoint

Huey Long once kidded Texas governor James Ferguson, saying, "If there had been a back door at the Alamo, there wouldn't have been a Texas." The governor shot back, "But there was a back door. That's why there's a Louisiana."

Long was assassinated not long after his filibuster. Surprisingly, his assassin was not someone who had to sit through his speech. Long's last words were, "God, don't let me die. I have so much left to do." It was true. He was planning on running for president in 1936, and he was so confident he'd win, he'd already started a book titled *My First Days in the White House*.

MR. INEXPLICABLE GOES TO WASHINGTON

Serving during the 1930s, representative Marion Zioncheck of Washington was one of the strangest congressmen ever. On the floor of the House, he once denounced a Texas colleague: "I shall put it on the record that the gentleman from Texas is a son of a Texan!"

Even weirder, the gentleman from Texas was angered by this remark!

Zioncheck also once left a gift for President Franklin Delano Roosevelt at the

White House: a black bag filled with Ping-Pong balls and empty beer bottles.

A SAD STORY

In 1979, in a law enforcement operation called "Abscam" (short for "Arab scam"), undercover agents posed as wealthy Arabs trying to bribe politicians with cash to get their votes. A number of representatives and a senator were convicted in Abscam, including Congressman Richard Kelly. After he was caught, Kelly was videotaped stuffing thousands of dollars in his pockets while saying, "If I told you how poor I am, you'd cry. I mean, the tears would roll down your eyes."

BAD MEN HAVE BAD EXCUSES

When Representative Daniel Rostenkowski of Illinois was accused of several corruption charges in 1994, he said, "I will fight these false charges and will prevail. I will wash away the mud that has been spattered upon my reputation. Some ask,

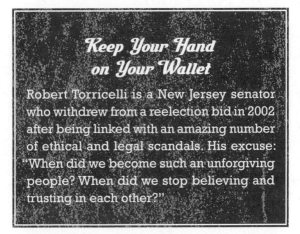

Keep Your Hand on Your Wallet

Robert Torricelli is a New Jersey senator who withdrew from a reelection bid in 2002 after being linked with an amazing number of ethical and legal scandals. His excuse: "When did we become such an unforgiving people? When did we stop believing and trusting in each other?"

'How could you have done these things?' The answer is simple. I didn't do them."

Rostenkowksi pled guilty. The judge sentencing him to seventeen months in jail said, "You shamelessly abused the institution you served." Rostenkowski's response: "I have served . . . with dignity, honor, and integrity." So much for public disgrace!

In 2006, Judge Eric Johnson sentenced White House adviser Claude Allen for shoplifting. The judge said, "You are a classic example, a fresh and enlightening example, that shame is not dead." Allen wept in court and insisted, "I did not realize or fully appreciate what was going on."

Too bad these guys never learned one of the first rules of brilliance. As Harry Truman's vice president, Alben Barkley, said, "If you have to eat crow, eat it while it's hot."

WRITERS AND ACTORS: THE WORST VILLAINS OF ALL!

In 1849, William Shakespeare and William Macready caused one of the bloodiest riots in United States history. These two Brits infuriated a mob of more than ten thousand New Yorkers outside the Astor Place Theatre. The evening would end with more than twenty people shot to death by soldiers.

To understand this bizarre incident, we have to remember that Shakespeare's plays were extremely popular throughout the United States in the 1800s. But while Americans enjoyed the Bard's plays, they resented the polished style of British actors. They seemed so snooty, so snobby . . . so *British*.

Noted Shakespearean actor William Macready just made things worse by writing things like, "[American] masses, rich and poor, are essentially ignorant or vulgar, utterly deficient in taste."

Macready was also involved in a very public feud with popular American actor Edwin Forrest. Americans were so mad at Macready, an audience member in Cincinnati threw a sheep carcass onstage while Macready was acting. (And to think I have trouble sneaking *popcorn* into the movies!)

Dead sheep aside, Macready came to New York to star in a production of *Macbeth* at the swankiest opera house in town. It was the perfect place for his style of thespianism, with a dress code that insisted on "freshly shaven faces, evening dress, fresh waistcoats, and kid gloves."

On May 7, a New York gang called the "B'hoys" attended a performance of Macready's *Macbeth*. The hoodlums interrupted Macready's acting by throwing chairs and vegetables onstage while shouting, "Three groans for the English bulldog!" (Sheesh, everyone's a critic.) Despite the chaos, Macready came back for another performance three nights later.

Not only were the B'hoys in attendance again, but a huge throng had gathered outside the theater to protest Macready. The crowd was rambunctious, and after three B'hoys were arrested inside the theater, chaos reigned. Paving stones poured through the theater's windows, the chandelier was broken, and theater-goers stampeded outside where they ran into the crowd. Arguments began. (*"It's pronounced 'Thee-AY-tuh'*... *AAAAH!"*). The New York militia was on the scene, trying to avoid getting hit by bricks and readying their bayonets.

Finally, a militia general cried, "Don't hit above the legs!" The idea was to open fire, but only to wound. But when the shooting was over, more than twenty people were found dead, and dozens more were injured. This was the first time in American history that a mob was fired on by an armed militia.

As for Macready, he finished the play that night in front of a nearly empty opera house and then sailed for home. He retired from the stage two years later. The Astor Place Theatre became known as "DisAster Place," and Shakespeare would never matter so much to so many Americans again.

MOTHER, MAY I?

New York has had plenty of criminal masterminds, but none with more estrogen coursing through her veins than "Mother" Frederika Mandelbaum (1818–1894). Serving as a "fence" (a middleman, er, mother, for stolen goods), Mother moved nearly $10 million from 1862 to 1882 alone. The *New York Times* wrote that she ran "the most notorious depot for stolen goods on the continent."

Among her keys to success was client loyalty. If one of her thieves was arrested, Mother posted bail for him. And if he got locked up anyway, Mother made sure there was another to replace him. She did this by running a school where street

245

kids learned the basics of lockpicking and pickpocketing.

When she was arrested in 1884 for her activities, Mother's son posted bail for her. Her home was constantly being monitored by detectives making sure she didn't flee the country, so she tricked them by sending out a servant disguised as herself. The servant led the detectives on a wild goose-chase for hours while Mother hopped in a carriage and made her way to Canada.

And in Canada Mother stayed, living the good life. She successfully fought off extradition attempts, and even snuck back into the United States for her daughter's funeral in 1891. A good businesswoman till the end, Mother Mandelbaum was the equivalent of a millionaire several times over upon her demise.

SO BRILLIANT, SO VILE

Thomas Edison was a brilliant inventor and a horrible man. When George Westinghouse introduced his new alternating current (AC) electrical system, it was in direct competition with Edison's own direct current (DC) business venture. To smear his rival's product, Edison tried to introduce a new word into the nation's vocabulary: "Westinghoused," meaning "electrocuted"!

Actually, AC was *less* dangerous than DC, but no matter. To further his campaign, Edison paid neighborhood kids to gather unwanted dogs and cats to be publicly electrocuted using AC power. In 1903, Thomas Edison even staged the electrocution of a Coney Island elephant named Topsy. The elephant had been sentenced to death for stomping on a human who fed her a lit cigarette. (Smoking really can kill you.)

Despite Edison's campaign, Westinghouse's

Tattoo You

Edison invented a tattooing machine that was the forerunner of those used in tattoo parlors today. The great inventor even had a tattoo of five spots on his forearm.

AC became the industry standard for electrical current.

THE WITCH OF WALL STREET

The saying "It takes money to make money" applied to Hetty Green (1834–1963), who was nicknamed the Witch of Wall Street. She took $1 million and turned it into what would be nearly two billion dollars in today's market. This may make her the richest woman the United States has ever seen!

But it took Hetty more than fifty years and incredible cheapness to do it. She was so tightfisted, when she pinched a penny,

she could make it howl like a banshee. And don't get me started on what she did to *nickels* . . . oh, it was horrible.

Hetty inherited her $1 million when she was twenty-one. That year, she supposedly refused to light her birthday candles because it would be wasteful! Through outstanding investments, her nest egg grew and grew to an astounding size. She kept track of her millions by spending most of her days dressed in rags inside her bank's vault. Yes, you could say that Hetty Green was absolutely fixated on money.

Despite her millions, she and her family lived in cheap boardinghouses around New York to avoid paying property taxes. All clothes were bought secondhand, and she reportedly rarely (if ever!) washed her underwear so that it would last longer. How cheap was she? She'd only buy broken cookies! (Really.) And one legend of her miserliness was that Hetty spent all night looking for something precious she'd misplaced: a two-cent stamp!

★ *HETTY'S FAVORITE MEALS: FOR LUNCH, OATMEAL WARMED OVER THE RADIATOR. FOR DINNER, BAKED ONIONS.*

There's nothing wrong with being frugal, but Hetty took it way too far. When her son hurt his knee, she refused to take him to a doctor for two years. When she finally gave in, it was only to a charity hospital that would provide free service. When a doctor recognized the millionaire and asked her to pay, Hetty refused.

And her son's leg had to be amputated.

Hetty went to the grave content in one matter. Since she had never owned property, the state of New York couldn't prove she was a resident, and so Hetty's estate didn't have to pay any taxes. The bad news was that she would be categorized in the *Guinness Book of World Records* as "the world's greatest miser."

Forgotten Brilliance

"WE ARE PERMANENTLY THE UNITED STATES OF AMNESIA." —*Gore Vidal*

American citizens have excellent memories for forgetting. That isn't always a bad thing; forgetting all about polyester leisure suits and hair metal is to be encouraged. But in the process, they have forgotten about some brilliant moments. For example, everyone knows that Alexander Graham Bell invented the telephone. It was a great success in his lifetime, and by 1880, there were sixty thousand telephones in use in the United States.

Special Delivery

How many stamps would it take to mail yourself?

That was the question facing Henry Brown in 1849. A slave in Richmond, Virginia, Brown came up with a first-class plan to mail himself to freedom.

He got a shipping crate large enough that he could just barely fit into it. Breathing holes were bored into it, and a local shopkeeper agreed to mail Brown in the crate to Philadelphia. Brown got into the crate, the lid was nailed shut, and off he went.

The total length of the trip was just over a day, but in that time, Brown was left upside down for hours. Luckily, on a steamboat, two men turned the crate right-side-up to use for a chair. After his arrival in Philadelphia, Brown eventually escaped to Great Britain, leaving Virginia far behind. He even got a cool nickname out of the endeavor: Henry "Box" Brown.

But we've forgotten that there was no agreement about what to say when picking up a phone. Alexander Graham Bell favored saying "Ahoy!" but I like the Italian style of saying "Pronto!" ("I am ready"). How cool would it have been if both of these had caught on?

PERSON 1: Pronto!

PERSON 2: Ahoy!

Back in the 1880s, most folks just lifted the receiver and waited for *something* to happen. Others favored just saying "What?" How good is a conversation going to be that starts that way?

PERSON 1: [Silence]

PERSON 2: What?

PERSON 1: [Pause] What yourself!

Underarm Paste 'n' Pepsi!

"Mum," a paste that was rubbed on a person's armpits, went up for sale in 1888. It was the first trademarked deodorant. And in the early 1890s, a man from North Carolina named Caleb Bradham named his new soft drink "Brad's Drink." Ho-hum. But when the name was changed to Pepsi in 1898, business picked up.

THE FIRST FLYING MACHINE

Around the year 1900, the twentieth century began! It was going to be a brilliant, gleaming new future with telephones, cars, and even flying machines. Who achieved the first controlled flight of an aircraft?

A. The Wright brothers in 1903.

B. The Ambidextrous Sisters in 1902.

C. Gustave Whitehead in 1901.

While the Wright brothers' nine-hundred-foot-long Kitty Hawk flight is more famous, historians frequently refer to inventor Gustave Whitehead's plane flight two years earlier. But nobody took a photo of Gustave's maiden voyage, a publicity mistake that the Wright Brothers would not make.

DON'T SLAM THE "Y"

Despite the gleaming new century, the political mood in the United States was sour. Russia's 1917 Bolshevik Revolution had Americans dreading communists, socialists, and union members. And just as paranoia was gripping the nation, a flood of overseas immigrants arrived.

And the anarchists, good grief, the *anarchists*! At that time, anarchists weren't fun-loving skateboarders innocently spray-painting graffiti. Nope, they were very serious about disrupting society. Anarchists had killed a French

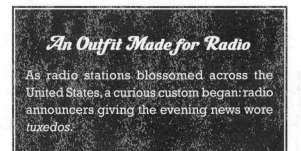

An Outfit Made for Radio

As radio stations blossomed across the United States, a curious custom began: radio announcers giving the evening news wore *tuxedos*.

president, an American president, and a Russian tsar. The anarchists had also made a number of unsuccessful assassination attempts on notables in and out of the United States and they'd successfully bombed London's Royal Greenwich Observatory.

This all led to the Sedition Act of 1918, which made it illegal to speak critically of the US government, its war effort, and even the YMCA. (No, I'm not kidding.)

But not all Americans subscribed to this fearful atmosphere. Pacifist Eugene Debs (1855–1926) was imprisoned for "obstructing the war effort" when he gave a speech opposing United States involvement in World War I. At his sentencing, Debs said:

YOUR HONOR, YEARS AGO I RECOGNIZED MY KINSHIP WITH ALL LIVING BEINGS, AND I MADE UP MY MIND THAT I WAS NOT ONE BIT BETTER THAN THE MEANEST ON EARTH. I SAID THEN, AND I SAY NOW, THAT WHILE THERE IS A LOWER CLASS, I AM

IN IT, AND WHILE THERE IS A CRIMINAL ELEMENT I AM OF IT, AND WHILE THERE IS A SOUL IN PRISON, I AM NOT FREE.

Inspirational! Yet when President Woodrow Wilson was asked if he would pardon Debs, he answered "Never!" What had Debs done to earn such hatred? Well, he had spent his life trying to draw national attention to the need for child labor laws, equal rights for women, and safety regulations for workers. What a jerk!

The problem Debs faced was that for many Americans, ANY criticism of the government was considered unpatriotic. Debs understood this, and at his trial,

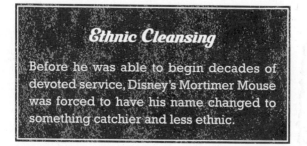

Ethnic Cleansing

Before he was able to begin decades of devoted service, Disney's Mortimer Mouse was forced to have his name changed to something catchier and less ethnic.

he reminded the jurors that trying to improve the nation was the very definition of "patriotism," and that the American founders had been branded criminals and traitors.

He was convicted and sentenced to ten years. His United States citizenship was also revoked. Yet Debs still ran for president from prison in 1920! Despite only being allowed to issue one written statement a week from his jail cell, Debs got nearly a million votes. This is still the best (and only!) showing by an incarcerated presidential candidate.

BUST A MOVE

Pioneering dancer Isadora Duncan was often accused of being dirty minded. She became famous for her innovative and unusual dance moves, which sometimes involved showing her bare arms, legs, and sometimes even a breast on stage. Heck, Isadora even danced when she was pregnant. *Sacré bleu!*

Duncan's last flamboyant gesture was in 1927. She got into an open convertible while wearing her trademark flowing scarf, which turned out to be a fatally unbrilliant accessory. A group of people had gathered to see the celebrity, and Duncan waved to them, saying, "Goodbye, my friends. I go to glory!"

Bye Bye American Pie

In 1982, a group celebrated new tax cuts by baking the world's largest apple pie. Free pieces of the pie were to be handed out at the Washington Monument. (It's symbolic!) But five protestors showed up and dove right into the huge pie. As shocked onlookers watched, the protestors rolled around in the pie pan, yelling, "It's all for me!" The protestors were arrested, and no one got ANY pie.

Conduct research on the best kind of pie to dive into. I'm guessing banana cream; lemon meringue might sting the eyes. Bake a large pie and test your theory.

With that, she drove off in style, her scarf flying in the wind behind her. The end of the scarf then wrapped around the car's rear axle. SNAP. Her neck was broken instantly. But her memory lived on! She had legally adopted six dance students, who carried on her style and beliefs.

BRILLIANCE IN THE DARK

By 1930, 70 percent of homes in the United States had electricity. But many of the homes a young Cesar Chavez (1927–1993) lived in were still wireless. Chavez was ten when his family lost its Arizona farm during the Great Depression. As an itinerant farm worker, the future union leader attended *thirty-eight* different schools by the end of his eighth-grade year. The experience would help inspire his future fights for the rights of migrant workers.

THE STATE OF WHAT MIGHT HAVE BEEN

In 1939, there were big changes in the air for the United States. Sure, World War

Backwoods Mixer

In the 1940s, a new soft drink appeared in Tennessee. Its label stated that it would "tickle your innards," and featured pictures of outhouses. Since it was designed to be mixed with homemade alcohol, there were also pictures of stills on these first bottles of . . . Mountain Dew!

II was about to start, but I'm referring to the creation of the newest American state, Absaroka.

If you've never heard of Absaroka, it's probably because you don't speak Crow. The word means "children of the large-beaked bird" in that language. Large beaked or not, Absaroka would have been big if it were officially given state-hood. The idea was to take large pieces of Montana, South Dakota, and Wyoming and create a state that shared its own special geography: grass-covered plains dotted with ranches.

Absaroka was no imaginary grass-covered Shangri La. Nope! The King of Norway made a state visit, and the larval state had its own governor and even a Miss Absaroka. But perhaps most important, Absaroka had its own license plates. It doesn't get more impressive than that!

OPENING ACT

As a child, Marian Anderson (1897–1993) had such an amazing voice, her friends and neighbors pooled their money to give her voice lessons. It was worth it. Anderson eventually went on a very successful tour of Europe, where the people didn't seem to mind the fact that she was black.

Back in the United States, Anderson was interested in performing for an integrated crowd in Washington, D.C. One problem: the Daughters of the American Revolution owned the town's best concert hall, and they had a "white artists only" policy. It didn't matter that Anderson had already performed at Carnegie Hall. The United States was segregated. It was legal and everything.

However, First Lady Eleanor Roosevelt resigned her DAR membership in protest. Roosevelt then helped arrange a free outdoors concert by Anderson near the

Lincoln Memorial. And so, in 1939, about seventy-five thousand people attended and millions more listened on radio as Anderson's deep contralto belted out her first number: "My Country, 'Tis of Thee."

Over twenty years later and at the same location, Martin Luther King Jr. quoted from the same song during his "I Have a Dream" speech.

STANDING ROOM ONLY

In 1954, the Supreme Court found that public institutions could no longer be segregated. In other words, blacks and whites were to share schools, libraries, and other public buildings. This created challenges for officials switching to the new system.

The folks running the public library in Danville, Virginia, were wondering how to change their policy when they saw something stunning. A small group of black youths came into the library, studied, and then left. It was unheard of!

Unluckily for the librarians, humorist Harry Golden had created something called the "Vertical Negro Plan." Golden's plan spoofed the whites who complained when blacks sat near them in restaurants, buses, or libraries. Since these same whites didn't complain when blacks STOOD near them, the "Vertical Negro Plan" stated that the key to integration was to remove all chairs from schools and libraries.

★ IN THE SEGREGATED SOUTH, ONLY BLACKS ACCOMPANYING WHITE CHILDREN COULD GET THE GOOD SEATS IN MOVIE THEATERS. THIS INSPIRED GOLDEN TO COME UP WITH HIS "WHITE BABY PLAN," WHEREIN BLACKS WHO WANTED TO GO TO THE MOVIES COULD "RENT" WHITE KIDS TO SIT WITH THEM.

The Danville librarians learned of the Vertical Negro Plan but weren't brilliant enough to see that it was a satire. And so library patrons were surprised to come in one day and find that EVERY chair had been removed from the Danville library. The chairs stayed gone (and everyone had to stay vertical) for about a week! Finally, someone explained to the embarrassed librarians that they'd been snookered, and the chairs returned.

Bananarama

In 1967, an underground newspaper called the *Berkeley Barb* published an article that made fun of the growing drug culture in the United States. The article claimed that banana peels contained a substance called "bananadine," which could be smoked. This would get the banana peel smoker high.

Although the article was very silly, it was widely reported on in the media. Soon, stoner wannabes were buying large quantities of bananas and smoking their peels.

GREEN LIGHT

The 1960s were a time of great upheaval for America. The Vietnam War, drug use, civil rights, and people with really long hair combined to throw the nation out of whack. In 1962—the year after Dow Corning released the first modern breast implants—a scientist named Rachel Carson published her book *Silent Spring*. The book convincingly showed that pesticides like DDT were destroying the ecosystem and affecting human health. This helped to focus the newborn environmental movement on pollution and being a watchdog of uncaring corporations.

Sadly, no watchdog was on hand in the 1970s to stop the unlikely team of glam-rocker David Bowie and Florence Henderson (of TV's *The Brady Bunch*). These two brilliant troublemakers managed to bring back James Polk's hairstyle from yesteryear: the mullet. The haircut subsequently became popular with hard rock fans in the 1980s.

269

Mullet Nicknames

shorty longback, Camaro crash-helmet, haircut o' death, Kentucky waterfall, hockey hair, Tennessee tophat, New Jersey neckwarmer, ape drape, Missouri compromise, Canadian passport

But it wasn't called the mullet yet. People in the South sometimes called stupid people "mullet-heads," but the haircut name seems to have come from a 1995 Beastie Boys song called "Mullet Head." (You saw that coming, right?) Sample lyrics: "You're coming off like you're Van Damme / You've got Kenny G, in your Trans Am / . . . #1 on the side and don't touch the back / #6 on the top and don't cut it wack, Jack."

As grunge emerged in the 1990s, mullets were derided as the symbols of the unhip—a hairstyle of the past. But the mullet has survived into the new millennium and continues to make appearances at ice hockey rinks, country western concerts, and in metalhead venues across the United States.

SAY IT LOUD! I HAVE IMMUNITY AND I'M PROUD!

In 1986, the city of Augusta, Georgia, honored hometown hero James Brown with "James Brown Appreciation Day." At the event, Congressman Doug Barnard praised Brown as "our number one ambassador."

The following year, Brown's wife, Adrienne, was pulled over for speeding and driving under the influence. Her lawyer came up with a creative defense: If James Brown was an ambassador, both he AND his wife should have "diplomatic immunity." (Diplomatic immunity protects ambassadors from going to jail while they're in foreign nations.) Nice try! But diplomatic immunity only works if the ambassador is from another country.

DREAM INTO ACTION

Congratulations, you finished this book! (Your brain must be pounding from all that you've learned.)

But you're not *really* finished. You are now obligated to share your newfound brilliance with others. To do so, immediately report to the nearest government office, brandish this book, and ask, "What can I do to help?" The civil servants will either put you in charge or call for security. Finding out which will be half the fun!